To Vicki

From
Demetrios

Happy & Joyous
2000

We, the People...

FORMATIVE DOCUMENTS OF AMERICA'S DEMOCRACY

Mayflower Compact
On Crimes and Punishments
Declaration of Causes
Declaration of Independence
Articles of Confederation
Constitution
Bill of Rights
Amendments
Emancipation Proclamation
Promissory Note

by ADOLPH CASO

Library of Congress Cataloging-in-Publication Data

We, the people-- : formative documents of America's democracy / by Adolph Caso
p. cm.
Includes bibliographical references and index.
ISBN 0-8283-2006-3 :
1. Beccaria, Cesare, marchese di, 1738-1794. Dei delitti e delle pene.
2. Criminal justice, Administration of--United States--History--Sources.
3. Beccaria, Cesare, marchese di, 1738-1794.
4. United States--Politics and government--Sources.
I. Title.
HV8661.C38 1995
364,973--dc20 95-3393
CIP

Branden Publishing Company Inc.
17 Station Street
PO Box 843 Brookline Village
Boston, MA 02147

Dedicated to the memory of:
CESARE BECCARIA,
who established the legal freedom and worthiness of men and women: "If a [state] be an association of families, there will be 20,000 men, and 80,000 slaves; if of men, there will be 100,000 citizens, and not one slave."

and to the memory of
my Parents

Mary Dyer was banned from Boston
and was hanged there because she was a Quaker.
(From *Mary Dyer--Biography of a Rebel Quaker* by Ruth Plimpton)

CONTENTS

FOREWORD

Although the words, "We, the People" suggest that the Constitution applies equally to all Americans, the attainment of that equality has fallen short for most people. And, despite many legislative attempts towards that end, the goal has remained elusive.

We, the People explores the potential meaning behind those words. This book, therefore, should serve as a stimulus to a better understanding of those words, and, through actions consonant to that meaning, we might work towards making America's Democracy attainable by the largest number possible.

In conjunction with the treatise *On Crimes of Punishments*, in form, content and execution, the documents herewith best represent America's democracy; for, they have guaranteed the people their sovereign rights to elect their named representatives, to hold them responsible and accountable for their actions while in office, and to limit, by various non-violent means, their stay in a single office or position.

These documents have allowed the American people to achieve, in governing themselves, standards of high democratic levels un-matched by any other people or nation. This attainment must be credited to those authors who, propelled by their various forms of idealism, were able to reduce their ideas into structured forms that are at the same time comprehensible and easy to execute.

The secret of this success cannot be ascribed to one single reason or cause. Yet, having emphasized, on a regular basis, the naming of individuals--be they signers of those documents, or those executing the laws--this naming of identified individuals rather than that of entities, supersedes all other considerations.

It is not the Republican or Democratic Party that executes the laws, but a named president elected by the people; it is not the Republican, Democratic, or Socialist Party that legislates, but named senators and representatives elected by the same people; likewise, it is a named judge (elected or appointed) that adjudicates. This practice, which runs the gamut of our democratic system, is the same at the local level as it is at the federal; it should also be applicable to other entities emanating from those documents.

A corporation can assume life only if it remains within the realm of the Constitution; if, for instance, it goes counter to the principle espoused in "We the People...", the corporation which discriminates could not exist. Nor should it exist if the delegation of responsibility is reverted to the corporation and not to named identifiable individuals.

Thus, the onus falls on the President, and not on the presidency, and likewise on down to the lowest political, civic, or commercial entity whose right to exist emanates from or through the Constitution.

The Founding Fathers were loathe to give special privileges to groups of people or to given entities; furthermore, as had happened in Europe and elsewhere in the world, they feared the rise of tyrannies by individuals who, for all kinds of reasons, had held and continued to hold the people in their strangleholds. Because of this fear--more intense than anything else, they sought to curb the power of those in "office" by various means, the most important being the checks and balances in the Constitution. They made sure not to create branches of government that might reduce in any significant way the various local autonomies; they refused to give the clergy special privileges as enjoyed in Europe; for basically the same reason, they also refused to recognize nobles or the nobility; and, by not establishing certain bureaus or departments such as that of education, they sought to deny those in office the possibility of using bureaus or departments as propaganda arms in order to prolong or extend their personal power beyond recognized established limits. In his anti-Hamiltonian editorial, Philip Freneau may have satirically said it best:

> *To be brief, let the whole be such a mystery that a few only can understand it; and let all possible opportunities and information fall in the way of these few, to clinch their advantages over the many."* (*American Issues*, p. 136)

In observing the success and longevity of our Democracy, one has to give credit to those authors; for, they cautiously and intelligently made sensible and pragmatic applications of their political principles. Their feats, as a result, remain unparalleled in the world.

Whether the goals of America's Democracy as expounded by the phrase, "We, the people..." have been achieved to the fullest possible extent, is another story. Certainly they were not achieved with the ratification of the Constitution, neither with the issuance of the Emancipation Proclamation, nor with the ratification of the 19th Amendment, nor with so much Civil Rights legislation. Yet, the Founding Fathers, knowing their own limitations, have projected their idealism through various documents, leaving to their progenitors to fulfill the nation's idealism through proper deeds of their own.

Achieving the ultimate goal, however, as espoused by "We the people..." has unfortunately remained elusive, and the "dream" of Dr. King remains a dream.

This may be due to special interest groups out to fulfill their restrictive programs without regard to the Constitution's supreme mandate; or, it may be the result of mis-application and mis-interpretation of our documents by well-meaning individuals in the public and private sectors. Blame, however, can extend to all other citizens who, for whatever reason, have not scrutinized for themselves our democracy's most important and easy-to-read documents. Blame can also be placed on entities as the *National Standards for United States History: Exploring the American Experience*. The group behind *National Standards* de-emphasizes the most cogent formative documents in the American experience by not mentioning the positive ones; yet, the same group emphasizes the more controversial aspects such as the ill-reputed Ku Klux Klan and Senator Joseph McCarthy, to name just a few, by over-citing them as though these individuals or entities are basic to the American experience.

This anthology makes possible the return to our origin--to the real and authentic documents that make America's Democracy what it is. They need our continuous reflection--here for us to re-consider and even to enjoy--and to do it without having to put up with the pains felt by the Founding Fathers when they came up with them. By reading these documents, we may discover the real meaning behind the words, "We, the People..." and begin fulfilling, in practical terms, the inherent mandate prescribed therein: the attainment of *the greatest happiness of the greatest number.*

CRITERIA FOR SELECTION

Although different documents and works were suggested, from the Code of Hammurabi up to the Marshall Plan, except for the Declaration of Independence and the Constitution with its Bill of Rights, and except for one or two individuals who confused the Articles of Confederation with the so-called Federalist papers, no one mentioned the Mayflower Compact, the Declaration of Causes or the Emancipation Proclamation. No one, except for a few in the legal profession, who had taken up the issue of capital punishment, had ever heard of Beccaria's *Treatise (Essay) On Crimes and Punishments*. Several, on the other hand, wanted to include the Magna Charta and put forward good arguments for its inclusion.

No one mentioned Thomas Paine's *Common Sense*; "'Tis time to part," he urged, and many adhered to his call. At the same time, he became such a critic as to distort truths and indiscriminately malign, without much justification, otherwise innocent people. Thomas Paine's attacks on George Washington, for example, were far more vehement that those seen on television today between party candidates running for the same office. Nevertheless, his pamphlet played a very important role in bringing about America's independence.

The goal of this book, therefore, is to bring together the documents and other corroborative works which have galvanized this continent--more specifically, items that were actually used to forge the nation that was to become the United States of America.

1. *MAYFLOWER COMPACT*

In the Mayflower Compact of November 11, 1620, the signers explain why they quit England, knowing all the while about the hardships ahead. Looking forward to their new settlement, they arrogated for themselves the right to "covenant and combine ourselves together into a civil body politic, for our better ordering and preservation, and furtherance of the ends aforesaid; and by virtue hereof do enact, constitute, and frame, such just and equal laws, ordinances, acts, constitutions, and offices, from time to time, as shall be thought most meet and convenient for the general good of the Colony unto which we promise all due submission and obedience."

The signers were leaving a nation governed by a monarchy guided by an established national (state) church. To see the word "constitution", therefore, becomes both brazen and promising at the same time. The signers may have been religious zealots at odds with the King and Church of England, but they were certainly clear in their undertakings and knowledgeable in the forms they were to design in order to govern themselves.

The original, herewith reproduced, is to be found among many other documents on the birth of this nation in the Archives of the State Library, Beacon Hill, Boston. The facsimile was made possible courtesy of the Library.

2. *ON CRIMES AND PUNISHMENTS*

The treatise *On Crimes and Punishments* by Cesare Beccaria (Marquis) from Milan, Italy, was widely used by our Founding Fathers. From George Washington to John Adams, to Thomas Jefferson, they all quoted extensively from this book. In England, Beccaria's treatise was also widely quoted, and came back to America through the works of individuals like William Blackstone, who became extremely important in matters of case law as adopted and adapted to American laws. This small book (*trattato* is often translated from the Italian into English as *essay* rather than *treatise*), is required reading in order to better understand America's form of government.

It was a best seller in the colonies, having been translated and published throughout the world, having had a major impact in England, France, Poland, Italy, Germany and even in Russia; yet, the book is woefully absent in today's writings.

3. *DECLARATION OF THE CAUSES...*

The Declaration of the Causes and Necessity of Taking up Arms, July 6, 1775, was the second such document by the Continental Congress (the first being the Declaration and resolves... issued about three months earlier). Although the issue of the King's abusive taxation was the single most important gripe of the colonists--the perennial cry against taxation without representation, as is known today--the distinguishing element of the Declaration of Causes lies in the new, revolutionary idea which claimed that governments exist for the people and not vice-versa: "But a reverence for our great Creator, principles of humanity, and the dictates of common sense, must convince all those who reflect upon the subject that government was instituted to promote the welfare of mankind, and ought to be administered for the attainment of that end."

This bold statement asserted what had already been discussed in Europe and in America, but never implemented in any definitive form. With the ensuing Declaration, which was to declare the Colonies' independence from England, the possibility of having a government existing for the people (and not the people existing for the government) began to take shape and to become reality. A government made to serve the people and not vice-versa is the cornerstone of America's Democracy.

In his Address, President John F. Kennedy challenged the American people in a very untraditional way: "ask not what your country can do for you; ask what you can do for your country." His recommendation may need to be re-assessed especially if compared to the Address of John Adams: "The declaration that our people are hostile to a government made by ourselves and for themselves, and conducted by themselves, is an insult." Adams' defense for the type of government he and his colleagues created is also defended by Abraham Lincoln as exemplified by his deeds in preserving the Union and in his words delivered at Gettysburg in 1863: that "this nation, under God, shall have a new birth of freedom, and that government of the people, by the people, and for the people shall not perish from the earth." Straying away from that cornerstone, therefore, should be forcefully avoided if Americans want to retain their democratic form of government and to remain steadfast in their basic character as individuals and as a people.

In the debates at the Convention of 1787, James Wilson of Pennsylvania, himself an immigrant from England, said it best: "The British Government cannot be our model. We have no materials for a similar one. Our manners, our laws, the abolition of enteils and of primogeniture, the whole genius of the people, are opposed to it."

Curiously, an extant Italian language version of this Declaration is to be found among the Jefferson papers at the Library of Congress, Washington, D.C., and offers several stylistic variations from the original published in Philadelphia.

4. *DECLARATION OF INDEPENDENCE*

The Declaration of Independence is the crowning glory of the Continental Congress. By reiterating the basic premise in the Declaration of Causes, and by adding that of independence with all of its ramifications, it specified the people's goal and described the means through which to achieve it. "We hold these truths to be self-evident, that all men are created equal, that they are endowed by their Creator with certain unalienable rights, that among these are life, liberty, and the pursuit of happiness.--That to secure these rights, governments are instituted among men, deriving their just powers from the consent of the governed,--that whenever any form of government becomes destructive of these ends, it is the right of the people to alter or to abolish it, and to institute a new government, laying its foundation on such principles, and organizing its powers in such form, as to them shall seem most likely to effect their safety and happiness." The language is felicitous, its content noble, its intent bold and revolutionary. With that kind of resolve, how could the "new" Americans not succeed!

5. *ARTICLES OF CONFEDERATION*

The Articles of Confederation were agreed to by Congress on November 15, 1777 and ratified on March 1, 1781: "to secure and perpetuate mutual friendship and intercourse among the people of the different States in this Union, the free inhabitants of each of these States, paupers, vagabonds and fugitives from justice excepted, shall be entitled to all privileges and immunities of free citizens in the several States; and the people of each state shall have free ingress and regress to and from any other State, and shall enjoy therein all the privileges of trade and commerce."

With this document, the Congress eliminated the "Colony" as a legal entity and established the "State". Then they formed a "perpetual union between the States of New Hampshire, Massachusetts [etc]." By respecting each state's "sovereignty, freedom, and independence," and by bringing them into a federation, in essence, they succeeded in what many smaller European republics and city states had failed to achieve: the establishment of a federal Republic composed of smaller ones. Strangely, it also made provisions for Canada's possible inclusion into the Union.

6. *THE CONSTITUTION*

Whereas, The Declaration of Independence was the crowning glory of the Continental Congress, The Constitution of the United States of America has achieved the envious distinction of being the longest living document through which a people, often from the remotest parts of the world, have allowed themselves to be guided and governed by it. Without a doubt, it is a miracle if we were to contrast it to other constitutions, active or extant.

The greater miracle is that it came about. The hurdles were enormous. With slavery permeating the southern states, the issue regarding a formula for representation was complex indeed. Yet, with slaves inhabiting several states, with women not suited for voting, and with many other non-white property owners, it is a wonder that those involved in the constitutional deliberations agreed to the following preamble: "We, the people of the United States, in order to form a more perfect union, establish justice, insure domestic tranquility, provide for the common defense, promote the general welfare, and secure the blessings of liberty to ourselves and our posterity, do ordain and establish this Constitution for the United States of America."

Although the implications behind those innocuous words may have been incomprehensible to many, to many, however they must have been palatable and inscrutable at the same time, and this may be the reason why the preamble achieved consensus, when, for reasons cited above, it should have been rejected.

How can the mandate of "We, the people" be collective and exclusively restrictive at the same time? "We, the people" connotes collectivism--a single political body comprised of all the people. Whoever the specific writers may have been, in succeeding to insert those words at the beginning of the Constitution, they accomplished the biggest coup of the convention. Those words contain the code of the writers' secret hope that, notwithstanding the social context of their time, which could not permit the fulfillment of the mandate, their goal would be fulfilled on a future day. That day may have come for many; it has yet to come for all.

7. *THE BILL OF RIGHTS*

The Bill of Rights, comprising the first ten articles (amendments) to the Constitution, became the vehicle for a dynamic democracy. It not only gave the Constitution continuous life, it also allowed for the implementation of the goal inherent in "We, the people".

Of the articles contained in the Bill of Rights, the first and second seem to have generated the greatest number of discussions and controversies. Yet, though the language seems rather clear, the subject treated in each has roots if not precedence in previous documents or in other deliberations.

With reference to the second article, "A well regulated Militia, being necessary to the security of a free State, the right of the people to keep and bear Arms, shall not be infringed" really deals with the issue on the use of arms and has two parts: arms needed by units of a militia for "the security of a free State," and arms needed by individuals for personal protection and as tools for acquiring food. One is organizational, the other is individual and both fall into complemental ratio according to individual need and societal changes. In those days, it was naturally necessary for individuals to bear arms; today, that requirement does not exist because guns are not mostly used for personal protection or to acquire food. Instead, they are used by one individual to kill another, all too often for no compelling reason. This article does not give carte blanche for the uncontrolled ownership of guns because our individual situations are no longer similar to those of the days of our Founding Fathers.

As for religion, all European nations had, what has come to be known as, a state or established church through which a given religion received state endorsement. The Founding Fathers knew too well the role that established churches had served. As the tool of government, oppression and repression in the name of God too often became commonplace practice. Not that, on the other hand, the authors wished to enhance the role of religion in any way. But when they prohibited Congress, and all other legislative bodies emanating from the Constitution, from "prohibiting the free exercise thereof", in essence, they allowed the enhancement of religion itself.

How could a state religion not be the arm of the government? The Magna Charta came into being precisely because King John wanted his own man to be the Archbishop of Canterbury. And it was Stephen Langton, who, appointed by the Pope according to church election procedures, succeeded in reducing John's power by leading the feudal barons in coming up with the Magna Charta, intended to favor, enhance and guarantee their status and that of the church. In the long run, however, King John won out. With the rise of the Anglican church, the Archbishop was appointed by the King or Queen--a practice that changed only in the latter part of the 20th century when Queen Elizabeth allowed the Bishop to be elected by his peers.

As for the Founding Fathers, these kinds of situations could only be prevented by prohibiting the establishment of a state church, and by guaranteeing its "free exercise thereof". They must have recognized the futility in legislating on things of religious faith. Even in the most disciplined of religions, there are always as many variations in practice and intent as there are members. However small, unanimity in any area is practically impossible. Legislating on issues as school prayer is tantamount to subverting the Constitution.

8. *AMENDMENTS TO THE CONSTITUTION*

These Articles of Amendment, generally considered those ratified after the first ten articles of the Bill of Rights, comprise Article XI ratified in 1794 to Article XXVI ratified in 1971. Several other amendments were also proposed but were not ratified, the latest being the ERA--Equal Rights Amendment.

The amendments, reflecting needs of an evolving society, keep the Constitution alive. Of these, the most important--because it complements the Preamble of the Constitution, is Article XIII which abolishes slavery and involuntary servitude. This Amendment was also the most painful to achieve.

Projected through a hard-fought Civil War that almost divided the country into two or more parts, the

Amendment took shape in the heart of Abraham Lincoln with his Proclamation, and finally ratified in 1865 as Article XIII. It logically brought about the following two amendments.

Articles XIV, which made "persons born or naturalized in the United States...citizens", also prohibited states from abridging or depriving "any person of life, liberty, or property". And, with Article XV, the citizens were granted the right to vote.

Thus, with these amendments, the fulfillment of the Constitution's Preamble comes closer and closer to full realization.

9. *EMANCIPATION PROCLAMATION*

The Emancipation Proclamation is the single most important document by an individual who, with one stroke of the pen, came closest to fulfilling the mandated democratic idealism of the Preamble. With the ratification of the Articles above, America came even closer. Yet, neither the heart of Lincoln nor the wisdom of the Legislature were enough to cut across human bias and racism, and it is doubtful that bias and racism will ever disappear. These human attributes of negativity in the form of skin colors or body shapes or gender are the driving force at many levels of society, equally practiced within and between the races. We are all guilty of it.

The attainment of our Constitution's mandate, therefore, remains elusive, in spite of individuals like

Beccaria, John Adams, James Wilson, James Madison, Thomas Jefferson, George Washington, Abraham Lincoln, Martin Luther King, to name a few. They represent the spark and the hope that one day, we may all realize our mandated democratic idealism in "We, the People...", to the extent that labels of religion, race, gender, and adult age will not be considered for employment in the private or public sector, or for participation in any organization emanating from the Constitution. The Emancipation Proclamation, therefore, has yet to be implemented. When that happens, the Constitution's mandate will have been fulfilled.

10. *PROMISSORY NOTE*

America came close to our Constitution's fulfillment in the 1960 decade when Martin Luther King, Jr. delivered his Promissory Note "I have a dream speech" of August 28, 1963 in which he gave meaning and direction to his Ghandian revolution of non-violence:

> *I have a dream that my four little children will one day live in a Nation where they will not be judged by the color of their skins, but by the conduct of their character.*

His words and his actions served to awaken some Americans to the original rights expressed in the Preamble of the Constitution. Yet, though much legislation passed on behalf of Civil Rights, progress was made at legal and theoretical levels; little progress has been made in achieving equitable, practical and wholesome coverage for a great number of Americans living as they do--whites, blacks, native Americans, and Hispanics alike. In view of the little substantive progress, one has to conclude that the changes, having benefitted few, have exacerbated the lot of many. Considering the opportunities that America offers, one has to ask why this is happening in view of America's wealth, the basic goodness of its people, and the guiding force inherent in the documents that make America's Democracy possible--why is racism so rampant!

Citing the Constitution and the Declaration of Independence, Dr. King claims for himself, for his "four little children" and for all of us the unalienable rights of life, liberty and the pursuit of happiness guaranteed by our documents.

Having created a revolution with his words and deeds, there followed a counter-revolution that has not yet abated. Dr King's supposed followers have created power blocks based on physical attributes rather than on "the conduct of...[one's] character." The counter revolution may have achieved some short-range goals. Surely, for the long range results, power blocks--be they of color, ethnicity, religion or gender, are doomed to failure. Rage should never replace vision. As for Dr. King, his revolution was based on vision; as for his followers, their counter revolution is based on rage and they are, unfortunately, insuring that those rights inherent in "We, the People" remain unattainable. Yet, the potentials are there, both for Dr. King's "four little children" and for all other children, because when equal rights are denied to one, they are denied to all, and the "dream" un-necessarily remains a dream.

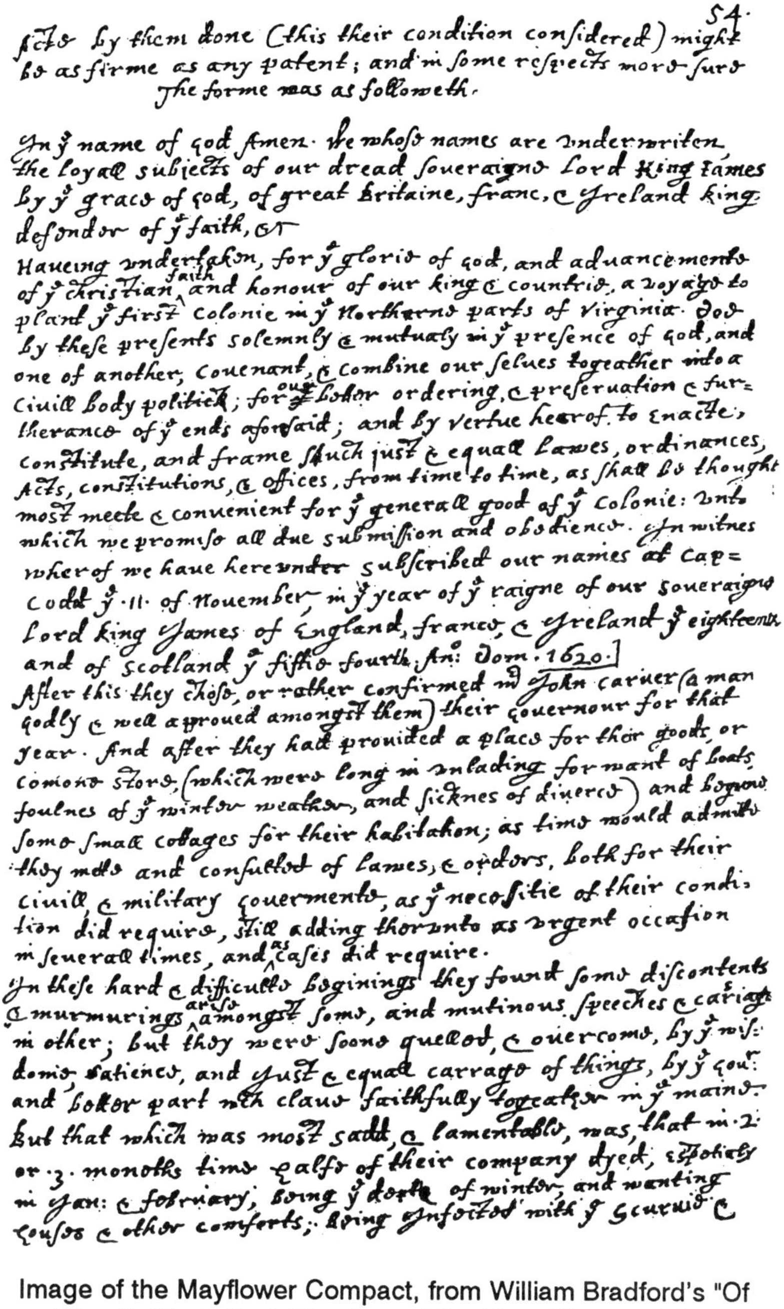

Acts by them done (this their condition considered) might 54.
be as firme as any patent; and in some respects more sure.
The forme was as followeth.

In ye name of god Amen. We whose names are underwriten,
the loyall subjects of our dread soveraigne Lord King James
by ye grace of god, of great Britaine, franc, & Ireland king,
defender of ye faith, &c
Haveing undertaken, for ye glorie of god, and advancemente
of ye christian faith and honour of our king & countrie, a voyage to
plant ye first colonie in ye Northerne parts of Virginia. doe
by these presents solemnly & mutualy in ye presence of God, and
one of another, covenant, & combine our selves togeather into a
civill body politick; for our better ordering, & preservation & fur=
therance of ye ends aforesaid; and by vertue hearof to enacte,
constitute, and frame shuch just & equall lawes, ordinances,
Acts, constitutions, & offices, from time to time, as shall be thought
most meete & convenient for ye generall good of ye Colonie: unto
which we promise all due submission and obedience. In witnes
wherof we have hereunder subscribed our names at Cap=
Codd ye .11. of November, in ye year of ye raigne of our soveraigne
Lord King James of England, France, & Ireland ye eighteenth
and of Scotland ye fiftie fourth. Ano: Dom. 1620.]
After this they chose, or rather confirmed Mr John Carver (a man
godly & well approoved amongst them) their Governour for that
year. And after they had provided a place for their goods, or
comone store, (which were long in unlading for want of boats,
foulnes of ye winter weather, and sicknes of diverce) and begune
some small cottages for their habitation; as time would admitte
they mette and consulted of lawes, & orders, both for their
civill & military governmente, as ye necessitie of their condi=
tion did require, still adding therunto as urgent occasion
in severall times, and as cases did require.
In these hard & difficulte beginings they found some discontents
& murmurings arise amongst some, and mutinous speeches & carriags
in other; but they were soone quelled, & overcome, by ye wis=
dome, patience, and just & equall carrage of things, by ye Govr
and better part wch clave faithfully togeather in ye maine.
But that which was most sadd, & lamentable, was, that in .2.
or .3. moneths time halfe of their company dyed, espetialy
in Jan: & February, being ye depth of winter, and wanting
houses & other comforts; being infected with ye scurvie &

Image of the Mayflower Compact, from William Bradford's "Of Plimoth Plantation" (*Courtesy of the State Library of MA*)

MAYFLOWER COMPACT
November 11, 1620

In the name of God, Amen. We, whose names are underwritten, the loyal subjects of our dread sovereigne Lord King James, by the Grace of God, of Great Britaine, France, and Ireland king, defender of the faith, having undertaken for the glory of God, and advancement of the Christian faith, and the honor of our king and country, a voyage to plant the first colony in the Northerne parts of Virginia, doe, by these presents, solemnly and mutually in the presence of God and one another, covenant and combine ourselves together into a civil body politick, for our better ordering and preservation, and furtherance of the ends aforesaid; and by virtue hereof do enact, constitute, and frame, such just and equal laws, ordinances, acts, constitutions, and offices, from time to time, as shall be thought most meet and convenient for the general good of the Colonie unto which we promise all due submission and obedience. In witness whereof we have hereunto subscribed our names at Cap-Cod the llth of November, in the reign of our sovereigne lord, King James of England, France, and Ireland, the eighteenth and of Scotland, the fifty-fourth. Anno. Domini, 1620.

Mr. John Carver	Mr. Stephen Hopkins
Mr. William Bradford	Digery Priest
Mr. Edward Winslow	Thomas Williams
Mr. William Brewster	Gilbert Winslow
Isaac Allerton	Edmund Margesson
Miles Standish	Peter Brown
John Alden	Richard Bitteridge
John Turner	George Soule
Francis Eaton	Edward Tilly
James Chilton	John Tilly
John Craxton	Francis Cooke
John Billington	Thomas Rogers
Joses Fletcher	Thomas Tinker
John Goodman	John Ridgate
Mr. Samuel Fuller	Edward Fuller
Mr. Christopher Martin	Richard Clark
Mr. William Mullins	Richard Gardiner
Mr. William White	Mr. John Allerton
Mr. Richard Warren	Thomas English
John Howland	Edward Doten

Edward Liester

An Essay
ON CRIMES AND PUNISHMENTS

Translated from the Italian;
Translated from the French.
Fourth Edition

In all things, and especially in the most difficult ones, we cannot expect one to concomitantly sow and reap the harvest; but we must first make preparations, and allow that things reach maturity little by little. (Bacon)

LONDON
Printed for F. Newberry, at the Corner of
St. Paul's Church-Yard.
M DCC LXXV.

To The Reader

The bulk of traditional legal opinions which throughout Europe have unfortunately been called laws are based on some remnants of an ancient conquering people's laws that a prince from Constantinople had had compiled only about twelve centuries ago. Later, they were mixed with Longobardian rituals; now they are gathered into encyclopedic-type volumes by private and little known interpreters of these laws. That our very men committed to uphold the lives and fortunes of other men should do so by obeying laws based on a single opinion of a Carpzov or on an ancient usage mentioned by a Claro, or administer punishments with irate complacency as suggested by a Farinaccio is indeed a prevalent practice today as it is pernicious. These laws--drainage of the most barbarous of centuries, are examined in this book for that part that deals with criminal procedure whose disorders I wish to expose to those entrusted in securing the public's pursuit of happiness, in a style which should keep away only the illiterate and the ignoramus.

My simple inquiry of truth, and my freedom from public opinions with which this book is written, are the result of the sweet and enlightened manner in which I govern myself. The great monarchs and the benefactors of humanity who rule over us, should love the truth set forth herein with little fanatical vigor by this little known philosopher, reacting only against those who turn to force or to cunning industry and not to reason. The present disorders for the one who well examines all the circumstances, are the satire and the reproach of the past centuries and not of our century or of its legislators.

Therefore, let those who wish to honor me with their criticism begin to do so by understanding first the purpose of this work; for, far from trying to diminish legitimate authority, I wish to increase it more by the power of thinking than by that of force, especially if in the eyes of mankind authority is based on gentleness and on humanity. The misunderstood criticism published against this book is based on confused notions; as a result, this criticism forces me to interrupt for a moment my arguments to the enlightened readers in order to close once and for all any access to the errors of a timid zeal, or to the calumnies of malicious envy.

Moral and political principles which regulate mankind come from three sources: revelation, natural law, and man-made conventions. In its main purpose, the first principle cannot be compared to the other two; but they resemble each other in this respect--they are conducive to our happiness. To consider the relationship of the last does not exclude those of the first two. On the other hand, though the first two are divine and immutable, they were changed by man's false religions and by man's arbitrary notions of vice and virtue that have existed in our corrupt minds. So it seems necessary to examine separately and without any other consideration that which is generated by pure human conventions, either expressed or supposed by common necessity and utility--the idea being that every faction and every moral system must necessarily come to some sort of agreement; for it will always be a praiseworthy enterprise to force the most obstinate and incredulous of men to conform to those principles that induce men to live in a society. There are, therefore, three distinct classes of virtue and of vice: religious, natural, and political. These three classes must never be in contradiction among themselves; but not all the consequences and the obligation derived from one may be derived from the others. Not everything demanded by revelation can be demanded by the natural law; nor anything demanded by the latter is demanded by the pure social law. But is very important to separate that which results from the convention; that is, from the express or tacit agreements of men, because such is the limit of that force that can be legitimately exercised among men, without a special mandate of the Supreme Being. Therefore, the concept of political virtue can unblemishedly be called variable; the one of natural virtue would always be clear and manifest if it were not for the imbecility and passions of men that obscure it; and the one of religious virtue is always both one and constant because it is revealed immediately by God Himself and preserved by Him.

It would therefore be an error to attribute to those who speak of social conventions with their consequences principles contrary either to the natural law or to revelation, because the latter two do not enter into the discussion. It would further be an error for the one who, on speaking about a state of war before discussing the state of society, would give it the Hobbesian's sense that the natural state precedes the political state, instead of taking it as a fact born out of the corruption of human nature and from the lack of an expressed sanction. It would be another error to blame a writer (as though he were committing a crime) who considers the emanations of the social contract, not admitting those very emanations prior to the contract itself.

Both divine and natural justice are their essence immutable and constant because the relation between two similar objects is always the same. But human or political justice, being but a relation between the action and the various states of the society, that relation can vary according as that action becomes necessary or useful to that society; nor can that relation be well discerned unless it is analyzed by the proper individuals in all its complicated and ever-changing relationships of civil combinations. As soon as these principles--essentially distinct from one another are confused, there is no longer any hope to conduct logical arguments on public matters. It is up to the theologians to establish the boundaries of the just and the unjust, for that which deals with the intrinsic evil or goodness of the act: the establishment of the rapport of the just and the unjust--that is, the utility and the harm done to the society, belongs to the individual who deals in public matters; for, an object can never be prejudicial to another, because everyone can easily see how much pure political virtue must give way to the immutable virtue emanated by God.

Whosever--I repeat--should wish to honor me with his criticism, should not begin by supposing that I stand for destructive principles of either virtue in general or of religion. I have already demonstrated that such are not my goals. And, instead of making me out an atheist or of being one having seditious tendencies, the critics should rather attempt to find me out a bad logician or a freshman politician. Do not tremble over each of the sentences that upholds human interests. The critic should convince me, on the other hand, either of the uselessness or of the political harm that could grow out of my principles, and demonstrate to me the advantages of traditional practices. I have given public testimony of my religious beliefs and of my submission to my sovereign with my answers to the "Notes and observations". To answer to ulterior writings similar to those "Notes" would be superfluous. But whoever will write to me with that decency normally expected of honest men and of those enlightened ones who will dispense with my having to prove the first two principles, of whatever character they may be, the critic will find in me a man who will make every effort to answer all the questions. And above all, the critic will find in me a peaceful lover of truth.

Preface of the Translator To the First Edition

Penal laws, so considerable a part of every system of legislation, and of so great importance to the happiness, peace, and security of every member of society, are still so imperfect, and are attended with so many unnecessary circumstances of cruelty in all nations, that an attempt to reduce them to the standard of reason must be interesting to all mankind. It is not surprising, then, that this little book hath engaged the attention of all ranks of people in every part of Europe. It is now about eighteen months since the first publication; in which time it hath passed no less than six editions in the original language; the third of which was printed within six months after its first appearance. It hath been translated into French; that translation hath also been several times reprinted, and perhaps no book, on any subject, was ever received with more avidity, more generally read, or more universally applauded.

The author is the *Marquis* Beccaria, of *Milan*. Upon considering the nature of the religion and government under which he lives, the reasons for concealing his name are obvious; the whole was read, at different times, in a society of learned men in that city, and was published at their desire. As to the translation, I have preserved the order of the original, except in a paragraph or two, which I have taken the liberty to restore to the chapters to which they evidently belong, and from which they must have been accidentally detached. The French translator hath gone much farther; he hath not only transposed every chapter, but every paragraph in the whole book. But in this, I conceive, he hath assumed a right which belongs not to any translator, and which cannot be justified. His disposition may appear more systematical, but certainly the author hath as undoubted a right to the arrangement of his own ideas, as to the ideas themselves; and therefore, to destroy that arrangement, is to pervert his meaning, if he had any meaning in his plan, the contrary to which can hardly be supposed.

With regard to the commentary, attributed to Mons. de Voltaire, my only authority for supposing it his, is the voice of the public, which indeed is the only authority we have for most of his works. Let those who are acquainted with the peculiarity of his manner judge for themselves.

The facts above-mentioned would preclude all apology for this translation, if any apology were necessary, for translating into our language, a work which, from the nature of the subject, must be interesting to every nation; but must be particularly acceptable to the English, from the eloquent and forcible manner in which the author pleads the cause of liberty, benevolence and humanity. It may however be objected, that a treatise of this kind is useless in England, where, from the excellence of our laws and government, no examples of cruelty or oppression are to be found. But it must also be allowed, that much is still wanting to perfect our system of legislation: the confinement of debtors, the filth and horror of our prisons, the cruelty of jailers, and the extortion of the petty officers of justice, to all which may be added the melancholy reflection, that the number of criminals put to death in England is much greater than in any other part of Europe, are considerations which will sufficiently answer every objection. These are my only reasons for endeavoring to diffuse the knowledge of the useful truths contained in this little essay; and I say, with my author, that if I can be instrumental in rescuing a single victim from the hands of tyranny or ignorance, his transports will sufficiently console me for the contempt of all mankind.

INTRODUCTION

In every human society, there is an effort continually tending to confer on one part the height of power and happiness, and to reduce the other to the extreme of weakness and misery. The intent of good laws is to oppose this effort, and to diffuse their influence universally, and equally. But men generally abandon the care of their most important concerns to the uncertain prudence and discretion of those, whose interest it is to reject the best, and wisest institutions; and it is not till they have been led into a thousand mistakes in matters, the most essential to their lives and liberties, and are weary of suffering, that they can be induced to apply a remedy to the evils, with which they are oppressed. It is then they begin to conceive, and acknowledge the most palpable truths, which, from their very simplicity, commonly escape vulgar minds incapable of analyzing objects, accustomed to receive impressions without distinction, and to be determined rather by the opinions of others, than by the result of their own examination.

If we look into history we shall find, that laws, which are, or ought to be, conventions between men in a state of freedom, have been, for the most part, the work of the passions of a few, or the consequences of a fortuitous, or temporary necessity; not dictated by a cool examiner of human nature, who knew how to collect in one point, the actions of a multitude, and had this only end in view, *the greatest happiness of the greatest number*. Happy are those few nations, who have not waited, till the slow succession of human vicissitudes, should, from the extremity of evil, produce a transition to good; but, by prudent laws, have facilitated the progress from one to the other! And how great are the obligations due from mankind to that philosopher, who from the obscurity of his closet, had the courage to scatter amongst the multitude, the seeds of useful truths, so long unfruitful!

The art of printing has diffused the knowledge of those philosophical truths, by which the relations between sovereigns and their subjects, and between nations, are discovered. By this knowledge, commerce is animated, and there has sprung up a spirit of emulation, and industry, worthy of rational beings. These are the produce of this enlightened age; but the cruelty of punishments, and the irregularity of proceeding in criminal cases, so principal a part of the legislation, and so much neglected throughout Europe, has hardly ever been called in question. Errors, accumulated through many centuries, have never yet been exposed by ascending to general principles; nor has the force of acknowledged truths been ever opposed to the unbounded licentiousness of ill-directed power, which has continually produced so many authorized examples of the most unfeeling barbarity. Surely, the groans of the weak, sacrificed to the cruel ignorance, and indolence of the powerful; the barbarous torments lavished, and multiplied with useless severity, for crimes either not proved, or in their nature impossible; the filth and horrors of a prison, increased by the most cruel tormentor of the miserable, uncertainty, ought to have roused the attention of those whose business is to direct the opinions of mankind.

The immortal Montesquieu has but slightly touched on this subject. Truth, which is eternally the same, has obliged me to follow the steps of that great man: but the studious part of mankind, for whom I write, will easily distinguish the superstructure from the foundation. I shall be happy, if with him, I can obtain the secret thanks of the obscure, and peaceful disciples of reason, and philosophy; and excite that tender emotion, in which sensible minds sympathize with him, who pleads the cause of humanity.

An Essay On Crimes and Punishments

Chapter 1

Of the Origin of Punishment

Laws are the conditions, under which men, naturally independent, united themselves in society. Weary of living in a continual state of war, and of enjoying a liberty which became of little value, from the uncertainty of its duration, they sacrificed one part of it, to enjoy the rest in peace and security. The sum of all these portions of the liberty of each individual constituted the sovereignty of a nation; and was deposited in the hands of the sovereign, as the lawful administrator. But it was not sufficient only to establish this deposit; it was also necessary to defend it from the usurpation of each individual, who will always endeavor to take away from the mass, not only his own portion, but to encroach on that of others. Some motives, therefore, that strike the senses, were necessary to prevent the despotism of each individual from plunging society into its former chaos. Such motives are the punishments established against the infractor of the laws. I say, that motives of this kind are necessary; because, experience shows, that the multitude adopt no established principle of conduct; and because, society is prevented from approaching to that dissolution, (to which, as well as all other parts of the physical, and moral world, it naturally tends) only by motives, that are the immediate objects of sense, and which being continually presented to the mind, are sufficient to counterbalance the effects of the passions of the individual, which oppose the general good. Neither the power of eloquence, nor the sublimest truths, are sufficient to restrain, for any length of time, those passions, which are excited by the lively impressions of present objects.

Chapter 2

Of the Right to Punish

Every punishment, which does not arise from absolute necessity, says the great Montesquieu, is tyrannical. A proposition which may be made more general, thus. Every act of authority of one man over another, for which there is not an absolute necessity, is tyrannical. It is upon this then, that the sovereign's right to punish crimes is founded; that is, upon the necessity of defending the public liberty, entrusted to his care, from the usurpation of individuals; and punishments are just in proportion, as the liberty, preserved by the sovereign, is sacred and valuable.

Let us consult the human heart, and there we shall find the foundation of the sovereign's right to punish; for no advantage in moral policy can be lasting, which is not founded on the indelible sentiments of the heart of man. Whatever law deviates from this principle will always meet with a resistance, which will destroy it in the end; for the smallest force, continually applied, will overcome the most violent motion communicated to bodies.

No man ever gave up his liberty, merely for the good of the public. Such a chimera exists only in romances. Every individual wishes, if possible, to be exempted from the compacts, that bind the rest of mankind.

The multiplication of mankind, though slow, being too great for the means, which the earth, in its natural state, offered to satisfy necessities, which every day became more numerous, obliged men to separate again, and form new societies. These naturally opposed the first, and a state of war was transferred from individuals to nations.

Thus it was necessity that forced men to give up a part of their liberty; it is certain then, that every individual would choose to put into the public stock the smallest portion possible; as much only as was sufficient to engage others to defend it. The aggregate of these, the smallest portions possible, forms the right of punishing: all that extends beyond this is abuse, not justice.

Observe, that by *justice* I understand nothing more, than that bond, which is necessary to keep the interest of individuals united; without which, men would return to their original state of barbarity. All punishments, which exceed the necessity of preserving this bond, are in their nature unjust. We should be cautious how we associate with the word *justice*, an idea of any thing real, such as a physical power, or a being that actually exists. I do not, by any means, speak of the justice of God, which is another kind, and refers immediately to rewards and punishments in a life to come.

Chapter 3

Consequences of the Foregoing Principles

The laws only can determine the punishment of crimes; and the authority of making penal laws can only reside with the legislator, who represents the whole society, united by the social compact. No magistrate then (as he is one of the society) can, with justice, inflict on any other member of the same society, punishment, that is not ordained by the laws. But as a punishment, increased beyond the degree fixed by the law, is the just punishment, with the addition of another; it follows that no magistrate, even under a pretence of zeal, or the public good, should increase the punishment already determined by the laws.

If every individual be bound to society, society is equally bound to him, by a contract, which from its nature, equally binds both parties. This obligation, which descends from the throne to the cottage, and equally binds the highest, and lowest of mankind, signifies nothing more, than that it is the interest of all, that conventions, which are useful to the greatest number, should be punctually observed. The violation of this compact by any individual, is an introduction to anarchy.

The sovereign, who represents the society itself, can only make general laws, to bind the members; but it belongs not to him to judge whether any individual has violated the social compact, or incurred the punishment in consequence. For in this case, there are two parties, one represented by the sovereign, who insists upon the violation of the contract, and the other is the person accused, who denies it. It is necessary then that there should be a third person to decide this contest; that is to say, a judge, or magistrate, from whose determination there should be no appeal; and this determination should consist of a simple affirmation, or negation of fact.

If it can only be proved, that the severity of punishments, though not immediately contrary to the public good, or to the end for which they were intended, viz. to prevent crimes, be useless; then such severity would be contrary to those beneficent virtues, which are the consequence of enlightened reason, which instructs the sovereign to wish rather to govern men in a state of freedom and happiness, than of slavery. It would also be contrary to justice, and the social compact.

Chapter 4

Of the Interpretation of Laws

Judges, in criminal cases, have no right to interpret the penal laws, because they are not legislators. They have not received the laws from our ancestors as a domestic tradition, or as the will of a testator, which his heirs, and executors, are to obey; but they receive them from a society actually existing, or from the sovereign, its representative. Even the authority of the laws is not founded on any pretended obligation, or ancient convention; which must be null, as it cannot bind those who did not exist at the time of its institution; and unjust, as it would reduce men, in the ages following, to a herd of brutes, without any power of judging, or acting. The laws receive their force and authority from an oath of fidelity, either tacit, or expressed, which living subjects have sworn to their sovereign, in order to restrain the intestine fermentation of the private interests of individuals. From hence springs their true and natural authority. Who then is their lawful interpreter? The sovereign, that is, the representative of society, and not the judge, whose office is only to examine, if a man have, or have not committed an action contrary to the laws.

In every criminal cause the judge should reason syllogistically. The *major* should be the general law; the *minor*, the conformity of the action, or its opposition to the laws; the *conclusion*, liberty, or punishment. If the judge be obliged by the imperfection of the laws, or choose, to make any other, or more syllogisms than this, it will be an introduction to uncertainty.

There is nothing more dangerous than the common axiom: *the spirit of the laws is to be considered*. To adopt it is to give way to the torrent of opinions. This may seem a paradox to vulgar minds, which are more strongly affected by the smallest disorder before their eyes, than by the most pernicious, though remote, consequences produced by one false principle adopted by a nation.

Our knowledge is in proportion to the number of our ideas. The more complex these are, the greater is the variety of positions in which they may be considered. Every man hath his own particular point of view, and at different times, sees the same objects in very different lights. The spirit of the laws will then be the result of the good, or bad logic of the judge; and this will depend on his good or bad digestion; on the violence of his passions; on the rank, and condition of the accused, or on his connections with the judge; and on all those little circumstances, which change the appearance of objects in the fluctuating mind of man. Hence we see the fate of a delinquent changed many times in passing through the different courts of judicature, and his life and liberty, victims to the false ideas, or ill humor of the judge; who mistakes the vague result of his own confused reasoning, for the just interpretation of the laws. We see the same crimes punished in a different manner at different times in the same tribunals; the consequence of not having consulted the constant, and invariable voice of the laws, but the erring instability of arbitrary interpretation.

The disorders, that may arise from a rigorous observance of the letter of penal laws, are not to be compared with those produced by the interpretation of them. The first are temporary inconveniences which will oblige the legislator to correct the letter of the law, the want of preciseness, and uncertainty of which has occasioned these disorders; and this will put a stop to the fatal liberty of explaining; the source of arbitrary and venal declamations. When the code of laws is once fixed, it should be observed in the literal sense, and nothing more is left to the judge, than to determine, whether an action be, or be not conformable to the written law. When the rule of right which ought to direct the actions of the philosopher, as well as the ignorant, is a matter of controversy, not of facts, the people are slaves to the magistrates. The despotism of this multitude of tyrants, is more insupportable, the less the distance is between the oppressor and the oppressed; more fatal than that of one, for the tyranny of many is not to be shaken off, but by having recourse to that of one alone. It is more cruel, as it meets with more opposition, and the cruelty of a tyrant is not in proportion to his strength, but to the obstacles that oppose him.

These are means, by which security of person and property is best obtained; which is just, as it is the purpose of uniting in society; and it is useful, as each person may calculate exactly the inconveniences attending every crime. By these means, subjects will acquire a spirit of independence and liberty; however it may appear to those, who dare to call the weakness of submitting blindly to their capricious and interested opinions, by the sacred name of virtue.

These principles will displease those, who have made it a rule with themselves, to transmit to their inferiors the tyranny they suffer from their superiors. I should have every thing to fear, if tyrants were to read my book; but tyrants never read.

Chapter 5

Of the Obscurity of Laws

If the power of interpreting laws be an evil, obscurity in them must be another, as the former is the consequence of the latter. This evil will be still greater, if the laws be written in a language unknown to the people; who, being ignorant of the consequences of their own actions, become necessarily dependent on a few, who are interpreters of the laws, which, instead of being public, and general, are thus rendered private, and particular. What must we think of mankind, when we reflect, that such is the established custom of the greatest part of our polished, and enlightened Europe? Crimes will be less frequent, in proportion as the code of laws is more universally read, and understood: for there is no doubt, but that the eloquence of the passions is greatly assisted by ignorance, and uncertainty of punishments.

Hence it follows, that without written laws, no society will ever acquire a fixed form of government, in which the power is vested in the whole, and not in any part of the society; and in which, the laws are not to be altered, but by the will of the whole, nor corrupted by the force of private interest. Experience and reason shows us, that the probability of human traditions diminishes in proportion as they are distant from their sources. How then can laws resist the inevitable force of time, if there be not a lasting monument of the social compact?

Hence, we see the use of printing, which alone makes the public, and not a few individuals, the guardians and defenders of the laws. It is this art, which, by diffusing literature, has gradually dissipated the gloomy spirit of cabal and intrigue. To this art it is owing, that the atrocious crimes of our ancestors, who were alternately slaves, and tyrants, are become less frequent. Those who are acquainted with the history of the two or three last centuries, may observe, how, from the lap of luxury and effeminacy, have sprung the most tender virtues, humanity, benevolence, and toleration of human errors. They may contemplate the effects of, what was so improperly called, ancient simplicity, and good faith; humanity groaning under implacable superstition; the avarice and ambition of a few, staining, with human blood, the thrones and palaces of kings; secret treasons, and public massacres; every noble a tyrant over the people; and the ministers of the gospel of Christ, bathing their hands in blood. We may talk as we please of the corruption and degeneracy of the present age, but happily we see no such horrid examples of cruelty and oppression.

Chapter 6

Of the Proportion between Crimes and Punishments

It is not only the common interest of mankind, that crimes should not be committed, but that crimes of every kind should be less frequent, in proportion to the evil they produce to society. Therefore, the means made use of by the legislature to prevent crimes, should be more powerful, in proportion as they are destructive of the public safety and happiness, and as the inducements to commit them are stronger. Therefore there ought to be a fixed proportion between crimes and punishments.

It is impossible to prevent entirely all the disorders which the passions of mankind cause in society. These disorders increase in proportion to the number of people, and the opposition of private interests. If we consult history, we shall find them increasing, in every state, with the extent of dominion. In political arithmetic, it is necessary to substitute a calculation of probabilities, to mathematical exactness. That force, which continually impels us to our own private interest, like gravity, acts incessantly, unless it meets with an obstacle to oppose it. The effects of this force are the confused series of human actions. Punishments, which I would call political obstacles, prevent the fatal effects of private interest, without destroying the impelling cause, which is that sensibility inseparable from man. The legislator acts, in this case, like a skilful architect, who endeavors to counteract the force of gravity, by combining the circumstances which may contribute to the strength of his edifice.

The necessity of uniting in society being granted, together with the conventions, which the opposite interests of individuals must necessarily require, a scale of crimes may be formed, of which the first degree should consist of those, which immediately tend to the dissolution of society, and the last, of the smallest possible injustice done to a private member of that society. Between these extremes will be comprehended, all actions contrary to the public good, which are called criminal, and which descend by insensible degrees, decreasing from the highest to the lowest. If mathematical calculation could be applied to the obscure and infinite combinations of human actions, there might be a corresponding scale of punishments, descending from the greatest to the least; but it will be sufficient that the wise legislator mark the principal divisions, without disturbing the order, left to crimes of the *first* degree, be assigned punishments of the *last*. If there were an exact and universal scale of crimes and punishments, we should there have a common measure of the degree of liberty and slavery, humanity and cruelty of different nations.

Any action, which is not comprehended in the above mentioned scale, will not be called a crime, or punished as such, except by those who have an interest in the denomination. The uncertainty of the extreme points of this scale, has produced a system of morality which contradicts the laws; a multitude of laws that contradict each other; and many, which expose the best men to the severest punishments, rendering the ideas of *vice* and *virtue* vague and fluctuating, and even their existence doubtful. Hence that fatal lethargy of political bodies, which terminates in their destruction.

Whoever reads, with a philosophic eye, the history of nations, and their laws, will generally find, that the ideas of virtue and vice, of a good or a bad citizen, change with the revolution of ages; not in proportion to the alteration of circumstances, and consequently conformable to the common good; but in proportion to the passions and error by which the different law-givers were successively influenced. He will frequently observe, that the passions and vices of one age, are the foundation of the morality of the following; that violent passion, the offspring of fanaticism and enthusiasm, being weakened by time, which reduces all the phenomena of the natural and moral world so an equality, become, by degrees, the prudence of the age, and an useful instrument in the hands of the powerful, or artful politician. Hence the uncertainty of our notions of honour and virtue; an uncertainty which will ever remain, because they change with the revolutions of time, and names survive the things they originally signified; they change with the boundaries of states, which are often the same both in physical and moral geography.

Pleasure and pain are the only springs of action in beings endowed with sensibility. Even amongst the motives which incite men to acts of religion, the invisible legislator has ordained rewards and punishments. From a partial distribution of these, will arise that contradiction, so little observed, because so common; I mean, that of punishing by the laws, the crimes which the laws have occasioned. If an equal punishment be ordained for two crimes that injure society in different degrees, there is nothing to deter men from committing the greater, as often as it is attended with greater advantage.

Chapter 7

Of Estimating the Degree of Crimes

The foregoing reflections authorize me to assert, that crimes are only to be measured by the injury done to society. They err, therefore, who imagine, that a crime is greater or less, according to the intention of the person by whom it is committed; for this will depend on the actual impression of objects on the senses, and on the previous disposition of the mind; both which will vary in different persons, and even in the same person at different times, according to the succession of ideas, passions, and circumstances. Upon that system, it would be necessary to form not only a particular code for every individual, but a new penal law for every crime. Men, often with the best intentions, do the greatest injury to society, and with the worst do it the most essential services.

Others have estimated crimes rather by the dignity of the person offended, than by their consequences to society. If this were the true standard, the smallest irreverence to the divine Being ought to be punished with infinitely more severity, than the assassination of a monarch.

In short, others have imagined, that the greatness of the sin should aggravate the crime. But the fallacy of this opinion will appear on the slightest consideration of the relations between man and man, and between God and man. The relations between man and man are relations of equality. Necessity alone has produced, from the opposition of private passions and interests, the idea of public utility, which is the foundation of human justice. The others are relations of dependence, between an imperfect creature and his Creator, the most perfect of beings, who, has reserved to himself the sole right of being both law-giver, and judge; for he alone can, without injustice, be, at the same time, both one and the other. If he has decreed eternal punishments for those who disobey his will, shall an insect dare to put himself in the place of divine justice, or pretend to punish for the Almighty, who is himself all sufficient; who cannot receive impressions of pleasure, or pain, and who alone, of all other beings, acts without being acted upon? The degree of sin depends on the malignity of the heart, which is impenetrable to finite beings. How then can the degree of sin serve as a standard to determine the degree of crimes? If that were admitted, men may punish when God pardons, and pardon when God condemns; and thus act in opposition to the supreme Being.

Chapter 8

Of the Division of Crimes

We have proved, then, that crimes are to be estimated by *the injury done to society*. This is one of those palpable truths, which, though evident to the meanest capacity, yet, by a combination of circumstances, are only known to a few thinking men in every nation, and in every age. But opinions, worthy only of the despotism of Asia, and passions, armed with power and authority, have, generally by insensible, and sometimes by violent impressions on the timid credulity of men, effaced those simple ideas, which perhaps constituted the first philosophy of infant society. Happily the philosophy of the present enlightened age seems again to conduct us to the same principles, and with that degree of certainty, which is obtained by a rational examination, and repeated experience.

A scrupulous adherence to order would require, that we should now examine and distinguish the different species of crimes, and the modes of punishment; but they are so variable in their nature, from the different circumstances of ages, and countries, that the detail would be tiresome and endless. It will be sufficient for my purpose to point out the most general principles, and the most common and dangerous errors, in order to undeceive, as well those who, from a mistaken zeal for liberty, would introduce anarchy and confusion, as those, who pretend to reduce society in general to the regularity of a convent.

Some crimes are immediately destructive of society, or its representative; others attack the private security of the life, property, or honour of individuals; and a third class consists of such actions, as are contrary to the laws which related to the general good of the community.

The first, which are of the highest degree, as they are most destructive to society, are called crimes of *Leze-majesty* (High Treason). Tyranny, and ignorance, which have confounded the clearest terms and ideas, have given this appellation to crimes of a different nature, and consequently have established the same punishment for each; and on this occasion, as on a thousand others, men have been sacrificed, victims to a word. Every crime, even of the most private nature, injures society; but every crime does not threaten its immediate destruction. Moral, as well as physical actions, have their sphere of activity differently circumscribed, like all the movements of nature, by time and space; it is therefore a sophistical interpretation, the common philosophy of slaves, that would confound the limits of things, established by eternal truth.

To these succeed crimes which are destructive of the security of individuals. This security being the principal end of all society, and to which every citizen has an undoubted right, it becomes indispensably necessary, that to these crimes the greatest of punishments should be assigned.

The opinion, that every member of society has a right to do any thing, that is not contrary to the laws, without fearing any other inconveniences, than those which are the natural consequences of the action itself, is a political dogma, which should be defended by the laws, inculcated by the magistrates, and believed by the people; a sacred dogma, without which there can be no lawful society; a just recompense for our sacrifice of the universal liberty of action, common to all sensible beings, and only limited by our natural powers. By this principle our minds become free, active and vigorous; by this alone we are inspired with that virtue which knows no fear, so different from that pliant prudence, worthy of those only who can bear a precarious existence.

Attempts, therefore, against the life, and liberty of a citizen, are crimes of the highest nature. Under this head we comprehend not only assassinations, and robberies, committed by the populace, but by grandees and magistrates; whose example acts with more force, and at a greater distance, destroying the ideas of justice and duty among the subjects, and substituting that of the right of the strongest, equally dangerous to those who exercise it, and to those who suffer.

Chapter 9

Of Honour

There is a remarkable difference between the civil laws, those jealous guardians of life and property, and the laws of what is called *honour*, which particularly respects the opinion of others. Honour is a term, which has been the foundation of many long and brilliant reasoning, without annexing to it any precise, or fixed idea. How miserable is the condition of the human mind, to which the most distant, and least essential matters, the revolutions of the heavenly bodies, are more distinctly known, than the most interesting truths of morality, which are always confused and fluctuating, as they happen to be driven by the gales of passion, or received and transmitted by ignorance! But this will cease to appear strange, if it be considered, that as objects, when too near the eye, appear confused, so the too great vicinity of the ideas of morality, is the reason why the simple ideas, of which they are composed, are easily confounded; but which must be separated, before we can investigate the phenomena of human sensibility; and the intelligent observer of human nature will cease to be surprised, that so many ties, and such an apparatus of morality, are necessary to the security, and happiness of mankind.

Honour, then, is one of those complex idea, which are an aggregate not only of simple ones, but of others so complicated, that in their various modes of affecting the human mind, they sometimes admit, and sometimes exclude part of the elements of which they are composed; retaining only some few of the most common, as many algebraic quantities admit one common divisor. To find this common divisor of the different ideas attached to the word honour, it will be necessary to go back to the original formation of society.

The first laws, and the first magistrates, owed their existence to the necessity of preventing the disorders, which the natural despotism of individuals would unavoidably produce. This was the object of the establishment of society, and was either in reality, or in appearance, the principal design of all codes of laws, even the most pernicious. But the more intimate connections of men, and the progress of their knowledge, gave rise to an infinite number of necessities, and mutual acts of friendship, between the members of society. These necessities were not foreseen by the laws, and could not be satisfied by the actual power of each individual. At this epoch began to be established the despotism of opinion, as being the only means of obtaining those benefits, which the law could not procure, and of removing those evils, against which the laws were no security. It is opinion, that tormentor of the wise, and the ignorant, that has exalted the appearance of virtue above virtue itself. Hence the esteem of men becomes not only useful, but necessary to every one, to prevent his sinking below the common level. The ambitious man grasps at it, as being necessary to his designs; the vain man sues for it, as a testimony of his merit; the honest man demands it, as his due; and most men consider it as necessary to their existence. Honour, being produced after the formation of society, could not be a part of the common deposit, and therefore, whilst we act under its influence, we return, for that instant, to a state of nature, and withdraw ourselves from the laws, which, in this case, are insufficient for our protection.

Hence it follows, that in extreme political liberty, and in absolute despotism, all ideas of honour disappear, or are confounded with others. In the first case, reputation becomes useless from the despotism of the laws; and in the second, the despotism of one man, annulling all civil existence, reduces the rest to a precarious and temporary personality. Honour then is one of the fundamental principles of those monarchies, which are a limited despotism, and in these, like revolutions in despotic states, it is a momentary return to a state of nature, and original equality.

Chapter 10

Of Duelling

From the necessity of the esteem of others, have arisen single combats, and they have been established by the anarchy of the laws. They are thought to have been unknown to the ancients; perhaps because they did not assemble in their temples, in their theaters, or with their friends, suspiciously armed with swords; and, perhaps, because single combats were a common spectacle, exhibited to the people by gladiators, who were slaves, and whom freemen disdained to imitate.

In vain have the laws endeavored to abolish this custom, by punishing the offenders with death. A man of honour, deprived of the esteem of others, foresees that he must be reduced, either to a solitary existence, insupportable to a social creature, or become the object of perpetual insult; consideration sufficient to overcome the fear of death.

What is the reason, that duels are not frequent among the common people, as amongst the great? Not only because they do not wear swords, but because, to men of that class, reputation is of less importance, than it is to those of a higher rank, who commonly regard each other with distrust and jealousy.

It may not be without its use to repeat here, what has been mentioned by other writers; *viz.* that the best method of preventing this crime is to punish the aggressor, that is, the person who gave occasion to the duel, and to acquit him, who, without any fault on his side, is obliged to defend that, which is not sufficiently secured to him by the laws.

Chapter 11

Of Crimes, Which Disturb Public Tranquillity

Another class of crimes is that which disturbs the public tranquillity and the quiet of the citizens; such as tumults and riots in the public streets, which are intended for commerce and the passage of the inhabitants; the discourses of fanatics, which rouse the passions of the curious multitude, and gain strength from the number of their hearers, who, though deaf to calm and solid reasoning, are always affected by obscure and mysterious enthusiasm.

The illumination of the streets, during the night, at the public expense; guards stationed in different quarters of the city; the plain and moral discourses of religion, reserved for the silence and tranquillity of churches, and protected by authority, and harangues in support of the interest of public, delivered only at the general meetings of the nation, in parliament, or where the sovereign resides; are all means to prevent the dangerous effects of the misguided passions of the people. These should be the principal objects of the vigilance of a magistrate, and which the French call *Police*; but if this magistrate should act in an arbitrary manner, and not in conformity to the code of laws, which ought to be in the hands of every member of the community, he opens a door to tyranny, which always surrounds the confines of political liberty.

I do not know of any exception to this general axiom, that *Every member of society should know when he is criminal, and when innocent*. If censors, and, in general, arbitrary magistrates, be necessary in any government, it proceeds from some fault in the constitution. The uncertainty of crimes hath sacrificed more victims to secret tyranny, than have ever suffered by public and solemn cruelty.

What are, in general, the proper punishments for crimes? Is the punishment of death really *useful*, or necessary for the safety or good order of society? Are tortures and torments consistent with *justice*, or do they answer the *end* proposed by the laws? Which is the best method of preventing crimes? Are the same punishments equally useful at all times? What influence have they on manners? These problems should be solved with that geometrical precision, which the mist of sophistry, the seduction of eloquence, and the timidity of doubt, are unable to resist.

If I have no other merit than that of having first presented to my country, with a greater degree of evidence, what other nations have written, and are beginning to practice, I shall account myself fortunate; but if, by supposing the rights of mankind and of invincible truth, I shall contribute to save from the agonies of death one unfortunate victim of tyranny, or of ignorance, equally fatal; his blessing and tears of transport, will be sufficient consolation to me for the contempt of all mankind.

Chapter 12

Of the Intent of Punishments

From the foregoing considerations it is evident, that the intent of punishments, is not to torment a sensible being, nor to undo a crime already committed. Is it possible that torments and useless cruelty, the instruments of furious fanaticism, or the impotency of tyrants, can be authorized by a political body? which, so far from being influenced by passion, should be the cool moderator of the passions of individuals. Can the groans of a tortured wretch recall the time past, or reverse the crime he has committed?

The end of punishment, therefore, is no other, than to prevent the criminal from doing further injury to society, and to prevent others from committing the like offence. Such punishments, therefore, and such a mode of inflicting them, ought to be chosen, as will make the strongest and most lasting impressions on the minds of others, with the least torment to the body of the criminal.

Chapter 13

Of the Credibility of Witnesses

To determine exactly the credibility of a witness, and the force of evidence, is an important point in every good legislation. Every man of common sense, that is, every one whose ideas have some connection with each other, and whose sensations are conformable to those of other men, may be a witness; but the credibility of his evidence will be in proportion as he is interested in declaring or concealing the truth. Hence it appears, how frivolous is the reasoning of those, who reject the testimony of women on account of their weakness; how puerile it is, not to admit the evidence of those who are under sentence of death, because they are dead in law; and how irrational to exclude persons branded with infamy: for in all these cases they ought to be credited, when they have no interest in giving false testimony.

The credibility of a witness, then, should only diminish in proportion to the hatred, friendship, or connections, subsisting between him and the delinquent. One witness is not sufficient; for whilst the accused denies what the other affirms, truth remains suspended, and the right that every one has to be believed innocent, turns the balance in his favor.

The credibility of a witness is the less, as the atrociousness of the crime is greater, from the improbability of its having been committed; as in cases of witchcraft, and acts of wanton cruelty. The writers on penal laws have adopted a contrary principle, viz. that the credibility of a witness is greater, as the crime is more atrocious. Behold their inhuman maxim, dictated by most cruel of imbecility. *In atrocissimis, leviores conjecturae sufficiunt & licet judici jura transgredi*. Let us translate this sentence, that mankind may see one of the many unreasonable principles to which they are ignorantly subject. *In the most atrocious crimes the slightest conjectures are sufficient, and the judge is allowed to exceed the limits of the law*. The absurd practices of legislators, are often the effect of timidity, which is a principal source of the contradictions of mankind. The legislators, (or rather lawyers, whose opinions, when alive, were interested and venal, but which after their death become of decisive authority, and are the sovereign arbiters of the lives and fortunes of men) terrified by the condemnation of some innocent person, have burthened the law with pompous and useless formalities, the scrupulous observance of which will place anarchical impunity on the throne of justice; at other times, perplexed by atrocious crimes of difficult proof, they imagined themselves under a necessity of superseding the very formalities established by themselves; and thus, at one time, with despotic impatience, and at another with feminine timidity, they transform their solemn judgments into a game of hazard.

But to return. In the case of witchcraft, it is much more probable, that a number of men should be deceived, than that any person should exercise a power which God hath refused to every created being. In like manner, in cases of wanton cruelty, the presumption is always against the accuser, for no man is cruel without some interest, without some motive of fear or hate. There are no spontaneous or superfluous sentiments in the heart of man; they are all the result of impressions on the senses.

The credibility of a witness may also be diminished, by his being a member of a private society, whose custom and principles of conduct are either not known, or are different from those of the people. Such a man has not only his own passions, but those of the society of which he is a member.

Finally, the credibility of a witness is null, when the question relates to the words of a criminal; for the tone of voice, the gesture, all that precedes, accompanies and follows, the different ideas which men annex to the same words, may so alter and modify a man's discourse, that it is almost impossible to repeat them precisely in the manner in which they were spoken. Besides, violent and uncommon actions, such as real crimes, leave a trace in the multitude of circumstances that attend them, and in their effects; but words remain only in the memory of the hearers, who are commonly negligent or prejudiced. It is infinitely easier then to found an accusation on the words, than on the actions of a man; for in these, the number of circumstances, urged against the accused, afford him the variety of means of justification.

Chapter 14

Of Evidence and the Proofs of a Crime, and of the Form of Judgment

The following general theorem is of great use in determining the certainty of a fact. When the proofs of a crime are dependent on each other, that is, when the evidence of each witness, taken separately, proves nothing; or when all the proofs are dependent upon one, the number of proofs neither increase nor diminish the probability of the fact; for the force of the whole is no greater than the force of that which they depend; and if this fails, they all fall to the ground. When the proofs are independent on each other, the probability of the fact increases in proportion to the number of proofs; for the falsehood of one does not diminish the veracity of another.

It may seem extraordinary, that I speak of probability with regard to crimes, which, to deserve a punishment, must be certain. But this paradox will vanish, when it is considered, that, strictly speaking, moral certainty is only probability; but which is called a certainty, because every man in his senses assents to it from an habit produced by the necessity of acting, and which is anterior to all speculation. That certainty which is necessary to decide, that the accused is guilty, is the very same which determines every man in the most important transactions of his life.

The proofs of a crime may be divided into two classes, perfect and imperfect. I call those perfect which exclude the possibility of innocence; imperfect, those which do not exclude this possibility. Of the first, one only is sufficient for condemnation; of the second, as many are required as form a perfect proof; that is to say, that though each of these, separately taken, does not exclude the possibility of innocence, it is nevertheless excluded by their union. It should be also observed, that the imperfect proofs, of which the accused, if innocent, might clear himself, and does not, become perfect.

But it is much easier to feel this moral certainty of proofs, than to define it exactly. For this reason, I think it an excellent law which establishes assistants to the principal judge, and those chosen by lot; for that ignorance, which judges by its feelings, is less subject to error, than the knowledge of the laws, which judges by opinion. Where the laws are clear and precise, the office of the judge is merely to ascertain the fact. If, in examining the proofs of a crime, acuteness and dexterity be required; if clearness and precision be necessary in summing up the result; to judge of the result itself, nothing is wanting but plain and ordinary good sense, a less fallacious guide than the knowledge of a judge, accustomed to find guilty, and to reduce all things to an artificial system, borrowed from his studies. Happy the nation, where the knowledge of the law is not a science!

It is an admirable law which ordains, that every man shall be tried by his peers; for when life, liberty and fortune are in question, the sentiments, which a difference of rank and fortune inspire, should be silent; that superiority with which the fortunate look upon the unfortunate, and that envy with which the inferior regard their superiors, should have no influence. But when the crime is an offence against a fellow subject, one half of the judges should be peers to the accused, and the other, peers to the person offended. So that all private interest, which, in spite of ourselves, modifies the appearance of objects, is counteracted, and nothing remains to turn aside the direction of truth and the laws. It is also just, that the accused should have the liberty of excluding a certain number of his judges. Where this liberty is enjoyed for a long time, without any instance to the contrary, the criminal seems to condemn himself.

All trials should be public, that opinion, which is the best, or perhaps, the only cement of society, may curb the authority of the powerful, and the passions of the judge; and that the people may say, "We are protected by the laws; we are not slaves:" a sentiment which inspires courage, and which is the best tribute to a sovereign, who knows his real interest. I shall not enter into particulars. There may be some persons who expect that I should say all that can be said upon this subject; to such, what I have already written must be unintelligible.

Chapter 15

Of Secret Accusations

Secret accusations are a manifest abuse, but consecrated by custom in many nations, where, from the weakness of the government they are necessary. This custom makes men false and treacherous. Whoever suspects another to be an informer, behold in him an enemy; and from thence, mankind are accustomed to disguise their real sentiments; and from the habit of concealing them from others, they at last even hide them from themselves. Unhappy are those, who have arrived at this point! Without any certain and fixed principles to guide them, they fluctuate in the vast sea of opinion, and are busied only in escaping the monsters which surrounded them; to those, the present is always embittered by the uncertainty of the future; deprived of the pleasures of tranquillity and security, some fleeting moments of happiness, scattered thinly through their wretched lives, console them for the misery of existing. Shall we, amongst such men, find intrepid soldiers, to defend their king and country? Amongst such men, shall we find incorruptible magistrates, who, with the spirit of freedom and patriotic eloquence, will support and explain the true interest of their sovereign; who, with the tributes, offer up at the throne the love and blessing of the people, and thus bestow on the palaces of the great and the humble cottage, peace and security; and to the industrious a prospect of bettering their lot, that useful ferment and vital principle of states?

Who can defend himself from calumny, armed with that impenetrable shield of tyranny, secrecy? What a miserable government must that be, where the sovereign suspects an enemy in every subject; and to secure the tranquillity of the public, is obliged to sacrifice the repose of every individual?

By what argument is it pretended, that *secret accusations* may be justified! The public safety, say they, and the security and maintenance of the established form of government. But what a strange constitution is that, where the government, which hath in its favor not only power, but opinion, still more efficacious, yet fears its own subjects? *The indemnity of the informer?* Do not the laws defend him sufficiently; and are there subjects more powerful than the laws? *The necessity of protecting the informer from infamy.* Then secret calumny is authorized, and punished only when public. *The nature of the crime.* If actions, indifferent in themselves, or even useful to the public, were called crimes, both the accusation and the trial could never be too secret. But can there be any crime, committed against the public, which ought not to be publicly punished? I respect all governments; and I speak not of any one in particular. Such may sometimes be the nature of circumstances, that when abuses are inherent in the constitution, it may be imagined, that to rectify them would be to destroy the constitution itself. But were I to dictate new laws in a remote corner of the universe, the good of posterity, ever present to my mind, would hold back my trembling hand, and prevent me from authorizing *secret accusations.*

Public accusations, says Montesquieu, are more conformable to the nature of a republic, where zeal for the public good is the principal passion of a citizen, than of a monarchy, in which, as this sentiment is very feeble, from the nature of the government, the best establishment is that of *commissioners*, who, in the name of the public, accuse the infractor of the laws. But in all governments, as well in a republic as in a monarchy, the punishment, due to the crime of which one accuses another, ought to be inflicted on the informer.

Chapter 16

Of Torture

The torture of a criminal during the course of his trial is a cruelty consecrated by custom in most nations. It is used with an intent either to make him confess his crime, or explain some contradictions, into which he had been led during his examination; or discover his accomplices; or for some kind of metaphysical and incomprehensible purgation of infamy; or, finally, in order to discover other crimes, of which he is not accused, but of which he may be guilty.

No man can be judged a criminal until he be found guilty; nor can society take from him the public protection, until it have been proved that he has violated the conditions on which it was granted. What right then, but that of power, can authorize the punishment of a citizen, so long as there remains any doubt of his guilt? This dilemma is frequent. Either he is guilty, or not guilty. If guilty, he should only suffer the punishment ordained by the laws, and torture becomes useless, as his confession is unnecessary. If he be not guilty, you torture the innocent; for in the eye of the law, every man is innocent, whose crime has not been proved. Besides, it is confounding all relations, to expect that a man should be both the accuser and accused; and that pain should be the test of truth, as if truth resided in the muscles and fibers of a wretch in torture. By this method, the robust will escape, and the feeble be condemned. These are the inconveniences of this pretended test of truth, worthy only of a cannibal; and which the Romans, in many respects, barbarous, and whose savage virtue has been too much admired, reserved for the slaves alone.

What is the political intention of punishments? To terrify, and be an example to others? Is this intention answered, by thus privately torturing the guilty and the innocent? It is doubtless of importance, that no crime should remain unpunished; but it is useless to make a public example of the author of a crime hid in darkness. A crime already committed, and for which there can be no remedy, can only be punished by a political society, with an intention, that no hopes of impunity should induce others to commit the same. If it be true, that the number of those, who from fear or virtue respect the laws, is greater than of those by whom they are violated, the risk of torturing an innocent person is greater, as there is a greater probability, that, *caeteris paribus*, an individual hath observed, than that he hath infringed the laws.

There is another ridiculous motive for torture, namely, *to purge a man from infamy*. Ought such an abuse to be tolerated in the eighteenth century? Can pain, which is a sensation, have any connection with a moral sentiment, a matter of opinion? Perhaps the rack may be considered as the refiner's furnace.

It is not difficult to trace this senseless law to its origin; for an absurdity, adopted by a whole nation, must have some affinity with other ideas, established and respected by the same nation. This custom seems to be the offspring of religion, by which mankind, in all nations, and in all ages, are so generally influenced.

We are taught by our infallible church, that those stains of sin, contracted through human frailty, and which have not deserved the eternal anger of the Almighty, are to be purged away, in another life, by an incomprehensible fire. Now infamy is a stain, and if the punishments and fire of purgatory can take away all spiritual stains, why should not the pain of torture take away those of a civil nature? I imagine, that the confession of a criminal, which in some tribunals is required, as being essential to his condemnation, has a similar origin, and has been taken from the mysterious tribunal of penitence, where the confession of sins is a necessary part of the sacrament. Thus have men abused the unerring light of revelation; and in the times of tractable ignorance, having no other, they naturally had recourse to it on every occasion, making the most remote and absurd applications. Moreover, infamy is a sentiment regulated neither by the laws nor by reason, but entirely by opinion. But torture renders the victim infamous, and therefore cannot take infamy away.

Another intention of torture is, to oblige the supposed criminal to reconcile the contradictions into which he may have fallen, during his examination; as if the dread of punishment, the uncertainty of his fate, the solemnity of the court, the majesty of the judge, and the ignorance of the accused, were not abundantly sufficient to account for contradictions, which are so common to men, even in a state of tranquillity; and which must necessarily be multiplied by the perturbation of the mind of a man, entirely engaged in the thoughts of saving himself from imminent danger.

This infamous test of truth is a remaining monument of that ancient and savage legislation, in which trials by fire, by boiling water, or the uncertainty of combats, were called *Judgments of God*; as if the links of that eternal chain, whose beginning is in the breast of the first cause of all things, could ever be disunited by the institutions of men. The only difference between torture, and trials by fire and boiling water is, that the event of the first depends on the will of the accused; and of the second, on a tact entirely physical and external: but this difference is apparent only, not real. A man on the rack, in the convulsions of torture, has it as little in his power to declare the truth, as in former times, to prevent without fraud the effects of fire or boiling water.

Every act of the will is invariably in proportion to the force of the impression on our senses. The impression of pain, then, may increase to such a degree, that occupying the mind entirely, it will compel the sufferer to use the shortest method of freeing himself from torment. His answer, therefore, will be in effect, as necessary as that of fire or boiling water; and he will accuse himself of crimes of which he is innocent. So that the very means employed to distinguish the innocent from the guilty, will most effectually destroy all difference between them.

It would be superfluous to confirm these reflections by examples of innocent persons, who, from the agony of torture, have confessed themselves guilty: innumerable instances may be found in all nations, and in every age. How amazing that mankind have always neglected to draw the natural conclusion! Lives there a man, who, if he have carried his thoughts ever so little beyond the necessities of life, when he reflects on such cruelty, is not tempted to fly from society, and return to his natural state of independence?

The result of torture, then, is a matter of calculation, and depends on the constitution, which differs in every individual, and is in proportion to his strength and sensibility; so that to discover truth by this method is a problem, which may be better solved by a mathematician than a judge, and may be thus stated. *The force of the muscles, and the sensibility of the nerves of an innocent person being given, it is required to find the degree of pain necessary to make him confess himself guilty of a given crime*.

The examination of the accused is intended to find out the truth; but if this be discovered, with so much difficulty, in the air, gesture, and countenance of a man at ease, how can it appear in a countenance distorted by the convulsions of torture. Every violent action destroys those small alterations in the features, which sometimes disclose the sentiments of the heart. These truths were known to the Roman legislators, amongst whom, as I have already observed, slaves only, who were not considered as citizens, were tortured. They are known to the English, a nation in which the progress of science, superiority in commerce, riches and power, its natural consequences, together with the numerous examples of virtue and courage, leave no doubt of the excellence of its laws. They have been acknowledged in Sweden, where torture has been abolished. They are known to one of the wisest monarchs in Europe, who, having seated philosophy on the throne, by his beneficent legislation, has made his subjects free, though dependent on the laws; the only freedom that reasonable men can desire in the present state of things. In short, torture has not been thought necessary in the laws of armies, composed chiefly of the dregs of mankind, where its use should seem most necessary. Strange phenomenon! that a set of men, hardened by slaughter, and familiar with blood, should teach humanity to the sons of peace.

It is also, that these truths were known, though imperfectly, even to those by whom torture has been most frequently practiced; for a confession made during torture is null, if it be not afterwards conformed by an oath; which if the criminal refuses, he is tortured again. Some civilians, and some nations, permit this infamous *petitio principii* to be only three times repeated, and others leave it to the discretion of the judge; therefore of two men equally innocent, or equally guilty, the most robust and resolute will be acquitted, and the weakest and most pusillanimous will be condemned, in consequence of the following excellent method of reasoning. *I, the judge, must find some one guilty. Thou, who art a strong fellow, hath been able to resist the force of torture; therefore I acquit thee. Thou, being weaker, hath yielded to it; I therefore condemn thee. I am sensible that the confession, which was extorted from thee, has no weight; but if thou dost not confirm by oath what thou hast already confessed, I will have thee tormented again.*

A very strange, but necessary, consequence of the use of torture, is, that the case of the innocent is worse than that of the guilty. With regard to the first, either he confesses the crime, which he has not committed, and is condemned; or he is acquitted, and has suffered a punishment he did not deserve. On the contrary, the person, who is really guilty, has the most favorable side of the question; for if he supports the torture with firmness and resolution, he is acquitted, and has gained, having exchanged a greater punishment for a less.

The law, by which torture is authorized, says, *Men, be insensible to pain. Nature has indeed given you an irresistible self-love, and an unalienable right of self-preservation; but I create in you a contrary sentiment, an heroical hatred of yourselves. I command you to accuse yourselves, and to declare the truth, midst the tearing of your flesh, and the dislocation of your bones.*

Torture is used to discover, whether the criminal be guilty of other crimes besides those of which he is accused; which is equivalent to the following reasoning. *Thou art guilty of one crime, therefore it is possible that thou mayst have committed a thousand others; but the affair being doubtful, I must try it by my criterion of truth. The laws order thee to be tormented, because thou are guilty, because thou mayst be guilty, and because I chouse thou shouldst be guilty.*

Torture is used to make the criminal discover his accomplices; but if it has been demonstrated that it is not a proper means of discovering truth, how can it serve to discover the accomplices, which is one of the truths required. Will not the man who accuses himself, yet more readily accuse others? Besides, is it just to torment one man for the crime of another? May not the accomplices be found out by the examination of the witnesses, or of the criminal; from the evidence, or from the nature of the crime itself; in short, by all the means that have been used to prove the guilt of the prisoner? The accomplices commonly fly, when their comrade is taken. The uncertainty of their fate condemns them to perpetual exile, and frees society from the danger of further injury; whilst the punishment of the criminal, by deterring others, answers the purpose for which it was ordained.

Chapter 17

Of Pecuniary Punishments

There was a time when all punishments were pecuniary. The crimes of the subjects were the inheritance of the prince. An injury done to society was a favor to the crown; and the sovereign and magistrates, those guardians of the public security, were interested in the violation of the laws. Crimes were tried at that time, in a court of exchequer, and the cause became a civil suit between the person accused and the crown. The magistrate then had other powers than were necessary for the public welfare, and the criminal suffered other punishments than the necessity of example required. The judge was rather a collector for the crown, an agent for the treasury, than a protector and minister of the laws. But, according to this system, for a man to confess himself guilty, was to acknowledge himself a debtor to the crown; which was, and is at present (the effects continuing after the causes have ceased) the intent of all criminal causes. Thus, the criminal who refuses to confess his crime, though convicted by the most undoubted proofs, will suffer a less punishment than if he had confessed; and he will not be put to the torture to oblige him to confess other crimes which he might have committed, as he has not confessed the principal. But the confession being once obtained, the judge becomes master of his body, and torments him with a studied formality, in order to squeeze out of him all the profit possible. Confession then is allowed to be a convincing proof, especially when obtained by the force of torture; at the same time that an extrajudicial confession, when a man is at ease and under no apprehension, is not sufficient for his condemnation.

All inquiries, which may serve to clear up the fact, but which may weaken the pretentious of the crown, are excluded. It was not from compassion to the criminal, or from considerations of humanity, that torments were sometimes spared, but out of fear of losing those rights, which at present appear chimerical and inconceivable. The judge becomes an enemy to the accused, to a wretch, a prey to the horrors of a dungeon, to torture, to death, and an uncertain futurity, more terrible than all; he inquires not into the truth of the fact, but the nature of the crime; he lays snares to make him convict himself; he fears, lest he should not succeed in finding him guilty, and lest that infallibility, which every man arrogates to himself, should be called in question.

It is in the power of the magistrate to determine, what evidence is sufficient to send a man to prison; that he may be proved innocent, he must first be supposed guilty. This is what is called an *offensive* prosecution; and such are all criminal proceedings, in the eighteenth century, in all parts of our polished Europe. The true prosecution, *for information*; that is, an impartial inquiry into the fact, that which reason prescribes, which military laws adopt, and which Asiatic despotism allow in suits of one subject against another, is very little practiced in any courts of justice. What a labyrinth of absurdities! Absurdities, which will appear incredible to happier posterity. The philosopher only will be able to read, in the nature of man, the possibility of there ever having been such a system.

Chapter 18

Of Oaths

There is a palpable contradiction between the laws and the natural sentiments of mankind, in the case of oaths, which are administered to a criminal to make him speak the truth, when the contrary is his greatest interest. As if a man could think himself obliged to contribute to his own destruction; and as if, when interest speaks, religion was not generally silent; religion, which in all ages hath, of all other things, been most commonly abused; and indeed, upon what motive should it be respected by the wicked, when it has been thus violated by those who were esteemed the wisest of men?

The motives which religion opposes to the fear of impending evil; and the love of life, are too weak, as they are too distant, to make any impression on the senses. The affairs of the other world are regulated by laws entirely different from those by which human affairs are directed; why then should you endeavor to compromise matters between them? Why should a man be reduced to the terrible alternative, either of offending God, or of contributing to his own immediate destruction? The laws which require an oath in such a case, leave him only the choice of becoming a bad christian, or a martyr. For this reason, oaths become, by degrees, a mere formality, and all sentiments of religion, perhaps the only motive of honesty in the greatest part of mankind, are destroyed. Experience proves their inutility; I appeal to every judge, whether he has ever known that an oath alone has brought truth from the lips of a criminal; and reason tells us it must be so; for all laws are useless, and in consequence, destructive, which contradicts the natural feelings of mankind. Such laws are like a dike opposed directly to the course of a torrent; it is either immediately overwhelmed, or, by a whirlpool formed by itself, it is gradually undermined and destroyed.

Chapter 19

Of the Advantage of Immediate Punishment

The more immediately after the commission of a crime, a punishment is inflicted, the more just and useful it will be. It will be more just, because it spares the criminal the cruel and superfluous torment of uncertainty, which increases in proportion to the strength of his imagination and the sense of his weakness; and because the privation of liberty, being a punishment, ought to be inflicted before condemnation, but for as short a time as possible. Imprisonment, I say, being only the means of securing the person of the accused, until he be tried, condemned, or acquitted, ought not only to be of as short duration, but attended with as little severity as possible. The time should be determined by the necessary preparation for the trial, and the right of priority in the oldest prisoners. The confinement ought not to be closer than is requisite to prevent his flight, or his concealing the proofs of the crime; and the trial should be conducted with all possible expedition. Can there be a more cruel contrast than that between the indolence of a judge, and the painful anxiety of the accused; the comforts and pleasures of an insensible magistrate, and the filth and misery of the prisoner? In general, as I have before observed, *The degree of the punishment, and the consequences of a crime, ought to be so contrived, as to have the greatest possible effect on others, with the least possible pain to the delinquent.* If there be any society in which this is not a fundamental principle, it is an unlawful society; for mankind, by their union, originally intended to subject themselves to the least evils possible.

An immediate punishment is more useful; because the smaller the interval of time between the punishment and the crime, the stronger and more lasting will be the association of the two ideas of *Crime* and *Punishment*; so that they may be considered, one as the cause, and other as the unavoidable and necessary effect. It is demonstrated, that the association of ideas is the cement which unites the fabric of the human intellect; without which, pleasure and pain would be simple and ineffectual sensations. The vulgar, that is, all men, who have not general ideas, or universal principles, act in consequence of the most immediate and familiar associations; but the more remote and complex only present themselves to the minds of those who are passionately attached to a single object; or to those of greater understanding, who have acquired an habit of rapidly comparing together a number of objects, and of forming a conclusion; and the result, that is, the action in consequence, by these means, becomes less dangerous and uncertain.

It is, then, of the greatest importance, that the punishment should succeed the crime as immediately as possible, if we intend, that in the rude minds of the multitude, the seducing picture of the advantage arising from the crime, should instantly awake the attendant idea of punishment. Delaying the punishment serves only to separate these two ideas; and thus affects the minds of the spectators rather as being a terrible fight, than the necessary consequence of a crime; the horror of which should contribute to heighten the idea of the punishment.

There is another excellent method of strengthening this important connection between the ideas of crime and punishment; that is, to make the punishment as analogous as possible to the nature of the crime; in order that the punishment may lead the mind to consider the crime in a different point of view, from that, in which it was placed by the flattering idea of promised advantages.

Crimes of less importance are commonly punished, either in the obscurity of a prison, or the criminal is *transported*, to give, by slavery, an example to societies which he never offended; an example absolutely useless, because distant from the place where the crime was committed. Men do not, in general, commit great crimes deliberately, but rather in a sudden gust of passion; and they commonly look on the punishment due to a great crime as remote and improbable. The public punishment, therefore, of small crimes, will make a greater impression, and, by deterring men from the smaller, will effectually prevent the greater.

Chapter 20

Of Acts of Violence

Some crimes relate to *person*, others to *property*. The first ought to be punished corporally. The great and rich should by no means have it in their power to set a price on the security of the weak and indigent; for the, riches, which under the protection of the laws, are the reward of industry, would become the aliment of tyranny. Liberty is at an end, whenever the laws permit, that, in certain cases, a man may cease to be a *person*, and become *a thing*. Then will the powerful employ their address, to select from the various combinations of civil society, all that is in their own favor. This is that magic art which transforms subjects into beasts of burthen, and which, in the hands of the strong, is the chain that binds the weak and incautious. Thus it is, that in some governments, where there is all the appearance of liberty, tyranny lies concealed, and insinuates itself into some neglected corner of the constitution, where it gathers strength insensibly. Mankind generally oppose, with resolution, the assaults of barefaced and open tyranny; but disregard the little insect that gnaws through the dike, and opens a sure, though secret passage to inundation.

Chapter 21

Of the Punishment of the Nobles

What punishment shall be ordained for the nobles, whose privileges make so great a part of the laws of nations? I do not mean to enquire whether the hereditary definition between nobles and commoners be useful in any government, or necessary in a monarchy; or whether it be true, that they form an intermediate power, of use in moderating the excesses of both extremes; or whether they be not rather slaves to their own body, and to others, confining within a very small circle the natural effects and hopes of industry, like those little fruitful spots, scattered here and there in the sandy deserts of Arabia; or whether it be true, that a subordination of rank and condition in inevitable, or useful in society; and if so, whether this subordination should not rather subsist between individuals, than particular bodies; whether it should not rather circulate through the whole politic, than be confined to one part; and rather than be perpetual, should it not be incessantly produced and destroyed. Be these as they may, I assert that the punishment of a nobleman should in no wise differ from that of the lowest member of society.

Every lawful distinction, either in honors or riches, supposes previous equality, founded on the laws, on which all the members of society are considered as being equally dependent. We should suppose that men, in renouncing their natural despotism, said, *the wisest and most industrious among us should obtain the greatest honors, and his dignity shall descend to his posterity. The fortunate and happy, may hope for greater honors, but let him not therefore be less afraid, than others, of violating those conditions on which he is exalted.* It is true indeed that no such decrees were ever made in a general diet of mankind, but they exist in the invariable relations of things; nor do they destroy the advantages, which are supposed to be produced by the class of nobles, but prevent the inconveniences; and they make the laws respectable by destroying all hopes of impunity.

It may be objected, that the same punishment inflicted on a nobleman and a plebeian, becomes really different from the difference of their education, and from the infamy it reflects on an illustrious family; but I answer, that punishments are to be estimated, not by the sensibility of the criminal, but by the injury done to society; which injury is augmented by the high rank of the offender. The precise equality of a punishment can never be more than external, as it is in proportion to the degree of sensibility, which differs in every individual. The infamy of an innocent family may be easily obliterated by some public demonstration of favor from the sovereign; and forms have always more influence than reason on the gazing multitude.

Chapter 22

Of Robbery

The punishment of robbery, not accompanied with violence, should be pecuniary. He who endeavors to enrich himself with the property of another, should be deprived of part of his own. But this crime, alas! is commonly the effect of misery and despair; the crime of that unhappy part of mankind, to whom the right of exclusive property (a terrible, and perhaps unnecessary right) has left but a bare existence. Besides, as pecuniary punishments may increase the number of robbers, by increasing the number of poor, and may deprive an innocent family of subsistence, the most proper punishment will be that kind of slavery, which alone can be called just; that is, which makes the society, for a time, absolute master of the person, and labor of the criminal, in order to oblige him to repair, by this dependence, the unjust despotism he usurped over the property of another, and his violation of the social compact.

When robbery is attended with violence, corporal punishment should be added to slavery. Many writers have shown the evident disorder which must arise from not distinguishing the punishment due to robbery with violence, and that due to theft or robbery committed with dexterity, absurdly making a sum of money equivalent to a man's life. But it can never be superfluous to repeat again and again, those truths of which mankind have not profited; for political machines preserve their motion much longer than others, and receive a new impulse with more difficulty. These crimes are in their nature absolutely different, and this axiom is as certain in politics, as in mathematics, that between qualities of different natures, there can be no similitude.

Chapter 23

Of Infamy, Considered as a Punishment

Those injuries, which affect the honour, that is, that just portion of esteem, which every citizen has a right to expect from others, should be punished with infamy. Infamy is a mark of the public disapprobation, which deprives the object of all consideration in the eyes of his fellow citizens, of the confidence of his country, and of that fraternity which exists between members of the same society. This is not always in the power of the laws. It is necessary that the infamy inflicted by the laws should be the same with that which results from the relations of things, from universal morality, or from that particular system, adopted by the nation, and the laws, which governs the opinion of the vulgar. If, on the contrary, one be different from the other, either the laws will no longer be respected, or the received notions of morality and probity will vanish in spite of the declamations of moralities, which are always too weak to resist the force of example. If we declare those actions infamous, which are in themselves indifferent, we lessen the infamy of those which are really infamous.

The punishment of infamy should not be too frequent, for the power of opinion grows weaker by repetition; nor should it be inflicted on a number of persons at the same time, for the infamy of many resolves itself into the infamy of none.

Painful and corporal punishments should never be applied to fanaticism; for being founded on pride, it glories in persecution. Infamy and ridicule only should be employed against fanatics: if the first, their pride will be over-balanced by the pride of the people; and we may judge of the power of the second, if we consider that even truth is obliged to summon all her force, when, attacked by error armed with ridicule. Thus by opposing one passion to another, and opinion to opinion, a wise legislator puts an end to the administration of the populace, occasioned by a false principle, the original absurdity of which is veiled by some well-deduced consequences.

This is the method to avoid confounding the immutable relations of things, or opposing nature, whose actions not being limited by time, but operating incessantly, overturn and destroy all those vain regulations, which contradict her laws. It is not only in the fine arts, that the imitation of nature is the fundamental principle; it is the same in sound policy, which is no other than the art of uniting, and directing to the same end, the natural and immutable sentiments of mankind.

Chapter 24

Of Idleness

A wise government will not suffer, in the midst of labor and industry, that kind of political idleness, which is confounded, by rigid declaimers, with the leisure attending riches acquired by industry, which is of use to an increasing society, when confined within proper limits. I call those politically idle, who neither contribute to the good of society by their labor, nor their riches; who continually accumulate, but never spend; who are reverenced by the vulgar with stupid admiration, and regarded by the wise with disdain; who, being victims to a monastic life, and deprived of all incitement to that activity which is necessary to preserve, or increase its comforts, devote all their vigor to passions of the strongest kind, the passions of opinion. I call not him idle, who enjoys the fruits of the virtues, or vices, of his ancestors, and in exchange for his pleasures, supports the industrious poor. It is not then the narrow virtue of austere moralists, but the laws, that should determine, what species of idleness deserves punishment.

Chapter 25

Of Banishment, and Confiscations

He who disturbs the public tranquillity, who does not obey the laws, who violates the conditions on which men mutually support and defend each other, ought to be excluded from society, that is, banished.

It seems, as if banishment should be the punishment of those, who being accused of an atrocious crime, are probably, but not certainly, guilty. For this purpose would be required a law, the least arbitrary, and the most precise possible; which should condemn to banishment, those who have reduced the community to the fatal alternative, either of fearing or punishing them unjustly; still, however, leaving them the sacred right of proving their innocence. The reasons ought to be stronger for banishing a citizen, than a stranger, and for the first accusation, than for one who hath been often accused.

Should the person, who is excluded for ever from society, be deprived of his property? This question may be considered in different lights. The confiscation of effects, added to banishments, is a greater punishment, than banishment alone; there ought then to be some cases, in which, according to the crime, either the whole fortune should be confiscated, or part only, or none at all. The whole should be forfeited, when the law, which ordains banishment, declares at the same time, that all connections, or relations, between the society and the criminal, are annihilated. In this case, the citizen dies; the man only remains, and with respect to a political body, the death of the *citizen* should have the same consequences with the death of the *man*. It seems to follow then, that in this case, the effects of the criminal should devolve to his lawful heirs. But it is not on account of this refinement that I disapprove of confiscations. If some have insisted, that they were a restraint to vengeance, and the violence of particulars, they have not reflected, that though punishments be productive of good, they are not, on that account, more just; to be just, they must be necessary. Even an useful injustice can never be allowed by legislator, who means to guard against watchful tyranny; which, under the flattering pretext of momentary advantages, would establish permanent principles of destruction, and to procure the ease of a few in a high station, would draw tears from thousands of the poor.

The law which ordains confiscations, sets a price on the head of the subject, with the guilty punishes the innocent, and by reducing them to the indigence and despair, tempts them to become criminal. Can there be a more melancholy spectacle, than a whole family, overwhelmed with infamy and misery, from the crime of their chief? a crime, which if it had been possible, they were restrained from venting, by the submission which the laws themselves have ordained.

Chapter 26

Of the Spirit of Family in States

It is remarkable, that many fatal acts of injustice have been authorized and approved, even by the wisest and most experienced men, in the freest republics. This has been owing to their having considered the state, rather as a society of *families*, than of *men*. Let us suppose a nation composed of an hundred thousand men, divided into twenty thousand families of five persons each, including the head or master of the family, its representative. If it be an association of *families*, there will be twenty thousand *men*, and eighty thousand *slaves*; if of *men*, there will be an hundred thousand citizens, and not one *slave*. In the first case, we behold a republic, and twenty thousand little monarchies, of which the heads are the sovereigns; in the second, the spirit of liberty will not only breathe in every public place of the city, and in the assemblies of the nation, but in private houses, where men find the greatest part of their happiness or misery. As laws and customs are always the effect of the habitual sentiments of the members of a republic, if the society be an association of the heads of families, the spirit of monarchy will gradually make its way into the republic itself, as its effects will only be restrained by the opposite interests of each, and not by an universal spirit of liberty and equality. The private spirit of family is a spirit of minuteness, and confined to little concerns. Public spirit, on the contrary, is influenced by general principles, and from facts deduces general rules of utility to the greatest number.

In a republic of families, the children remain under the authority of the father, as long as he lives, and are obliged to wait until his death for an existence dependent on the laws alone. Accustomed to kneel and tremble in their tender years, when their natural sentiments were less restrained by that caution, obtained by experience, which is called moderation, how should they resist those obstacles, which vice always opposes to virtue, in the languor and decline of age, when the despair of reaping the fruits is alone sufficient to damp the vigor of their resolutions?

In a republic, where every man is a citizen, family subordination is not the effect of compulsion, but of contract; and the sons disengaged from the natural dependence, which the weakness of infancy and the necessity of education required, become free members of society, but remain subject to the head of the family for their own advantage, as in the great society.

In a republic of families, the young people, that is the most numerous, and most useful part of the nation, are at the discretion of their fathers: in a republic of men, they are attached to their parents by no other obligation, than that sacred and inviolable one of mutual assistance, and of gratitude for the benefits they have received; a sentiment, destroyed not so much by the wickedness of the human heart, as by mistaken subjection, prescribed by the laws.

These contradictions between the laws of families, and the fundamental laws of a state, are the source of many others between public and private morality, which produce a perpetual conflict in the mind. Domestic morality inspires submission, and fear: the other, courage and liberty. That instructs a man to confine his beneficence to a small number of persons, not of his own choice; this, to extend it to all mankind; that commands a continual sacrifice of himself to a vain idol, called the *good of the family*, which is often no real good to any one of those who compose it; this teaches him to consider his own advantage without offending the laws, or excites him to sacrifice himself for the good of his country, by rewarding him beforehand with the fanaticism it inspires. Such contradictions are the reasons, that men neglect the pursuit of virtue, which they can hardly distinguish midst the obscurity and confusion of natural and moral objects. How frequently are men, upon a retrospection of their actions, astonished to find themselves dishonest?

In proportion to the increase of society, each member becomes a smaller part of the whole; and the republican spirit diminishes in the same proportion, if neglected by the laws. Political societies, like the human body, have their limits circumscribed, which they cannot exceed without disturbing their economy. It seems as if the greatness of a state ought to be inversely as the sensibility and activity of the individuals; if on the contrary, population and activity increase in the same proportion, the laws will with difficulty prevent the crimes arising from the good they have produced. An overgrown republic can only be saved from despotism, by subdividing it into a number of confederate republics. But how is this practicable? By a despotic dictator, who, with the courage of *Sylla*, has as much genius for building up, as that Roman had for pulling down. If he be an ambitious man, his reward will be immortal glory; if a philosopher, the blessings of his fellow-citizens will sufficiently console him for the loss of authority, though he should not be insensible to their ingratitude.

In proportion as the sentiments, which unite us to the state, grow weaker, those which attach us to the objects which more immediately surround us, grow stronger; therefore, in the most despotic government, friendships are more durable, and domestic virtues (which are always of the lowest class) are the most common, or the only virtues existing. Hence it appears how confined have been the views of the greatest number of legislators.

Chapter 27

Of the Mildness of Punishments

The course of my ideas has carried me away from my subject, to the elucidation of which I now return. Crimes are more effectually prevented by the *certainty*, than the *severity* of punishment. Hence in a magistrate, the necessity of vigilance, and in a judge, of implacability, which, that it may become an useful virtue, should be joined to a mild legislation. The certainty of a small punishment will make a stronger impression, than the fear of one more severe, if attended with the hopes of escaping; for it is the nature of mankind to be terrified at the approach of the smallest inevitable evil, whilst hope, the best gift of heaven, hath the power of dispelling the apprehension of a greater; especially if supported by examples of impunity, which weakness or avarice too frequently afford.

If punishments be very severe, men are naturally led to the perpetration of other crimes, to avoid the punishment due to the first. The countries and times most notorious for severity of punishments, were always those in which the most bloody and inhuman actions and the most atrocious crimes were committed; for the hand of the legislator and the assassin were directed by the same spirit of ferocity; which, on the throne, dictated laws of iron to slaves and savages, and in private, instigated the subject to sacrifice one tyrant to make room for another.

In proportion as punishments become more cruel, the minds of men, as a fluid rises to the same height with that which surrounds it, grow hardened and insensible; and the force of the passions still continuing, in the space of an hundred years, the *wheel* terrifies no more than formerly the *prison*. That a punishment may produce the effect required, it is sufficient that the *evil* it occasions should exceed the *good* expected from the crime; including in the calculation the certainty of the punishment, and the privation of the expected advantage. All severity beyond this is superfluous, and therefore tyrannical.

Men regulate their conduct by the repeated impression of evils they know, and not by those with which they are unacquainted. Let us, for example, suppose two nations, in one of which the greatest punishment is *perpetual slavery*, and in the other *the wheel*. I say, that both will inspire the same degree of terror; and that there can be no reasons for increasing the punishments of the first; which are not equally valid for augmenting those of the second to more lasting and more ingenious modes of tormenting; and so on to the most exquisite refinements of a science too well known to tyrants.

There are yet two other consequences of cruel punishments, which counter-act the purpose of their institutions, which was, to prevent crimes. The *first* arises from the impossibility of establishing an exact proportion between the crime and punishment, for though ingenious cruelty hath greatly multiplied the variety of torments, yet the human frame can suffer only to a certain degree, beyond which it is impossible to proceed, be the enormity of the crime ever so great.

The *second* consequence is impunity. Human nature is limited no less in evil than in good. Excessive barbarity can never be more than temporary; it being impossible that it should be supported by a permanent system of legislation; for if the laws be too cruel they must be altered, or anarchy and impunity will succeed.

Is it possible, without shuddering with horror, to read in history of the barbarous and useless torments that were coolly invented and executed by men who were called sages? Who does not tremble at the thoughts of thousands of wretches, whom their misery, either caused or tolerated by the laws, which favored the few and outraged the many, had forced in despair to return to a state of nature; or accused of impossible crimes, the fabric of ignorance and superstition; or guilty only of having been faithful to their own principles; who, I say, can without horror, think of their being torn to pieces with slow and studied barbarity, by men endowed with the same passions and the same feelings? A delightful spectacle to a fanatic multitude!

Chapter 28

Of the Punishment of Death

The useless profusion of punishments, which has never made men better, induces me to enquire, whether the punishment of *death* be really just or useful in a well governed state? What *right*, I ask, have men to cut the throats of their fellow-creatures? Certainly not that on which the sovereignty and laws are founded. The laws, as I have said before, are only the sum of the smallest portions of the private liberty of each individual, and represent the general will, which is the aggregate of that of each individual. Did any one ever give to others the right of taking away his life? Is it possible, that in the smallest portions of the liberty of each, sacrificed to the good of the public, can be contained the greatest of all good, life? If it were so, how shall it be reconciled to the maxim which tells us, that a man has no right to kill himself? Which he certainly must have, if he could give it away to another.

But the punishment of death is not authorized by any right; for I have demonstrated that no such right exists. It is therefore a war of a whole nation against a citizen, whose destruction they consider as necessary, or useful to the general good. But if I can further demonstrate, that it is neither necessary nor useful, I shall have gained the cause of humanity.

The death of a citizen cannot be necessary, but in one case. When, though deprived of his liberty, he has such power and connections as may endanger the security of the nation; when his existence may produce a dangerous revolution in the established form of government. But even in this case, it can only be necessary when a nation is on the verge of recovering or losing its liberty; or in times of absolute anarchy, when the disorders themselves hold the place of laws. But in a reign of tranquillity; in a form of government approved by the united wishes of the nation; in a state well fortified from enemies without, and supported by strength within, and opinion, perhaps more efficacious; where all power is lodged in the hands of a true sovereign; where riches can purchase pleasures and not authority, there can be no necessity for taking away the life of a subject.

If the experience of all ages be not sufficient to prove, that the punishment of death has never prevented determined men from injuring society; if the example of the Romans; if twenty years reign of Elizabeth, empress of Russia, in which she gave the fathers of their country an example more illustrious than many conquests bought with blood; if, I say, all this be not sufficient to persuade mankind, who always suspect the voice of reason, and who choose rather to be led by authority, let us consult human nature in proof of my assertion.

It is not the intenseness of the pain that has the greatest effect on the mind, but its continuance; for our sensibility is more easily and more powerfully affected by weak but repeated impressions, than by a violent, but momentary, impulse. The power of habits is universal over every sensible being. As it is by that we learn to speak, to walk, and to satisfy our necessities, so the ideas of morality are stamped on our minds by repeated impressions. The death of a criminal is a terrible but momentary spectacle, and therefore a less efficacious method of deterring others, than the continued example of a man deprived of his liberty, condemned, as a beast of burthen, to repair, by his labor, the injury he has done to society. *If I commit such a crime*, says the spectator to himself, *I shall be reduced to that miserable condition for the rest of my life*. A much more powerful preventive than the fear of death, which men always behold in distant obscurity.

The terrors of death make so slight an impression, that it has not force enough to withstand the forgetfulness natural to mankind, even in the most essential things; especially when assisted by the passions. Violent impressions surprise us, but their effect is momentary; they are fit to produce those revolutions which instantly transform a common man into a Lacedonian or a Persian; but in a free and quiet government they ought to be rather frequent than strong.

The execution of a criminal is, to the multitude, a spectacle, which in some excites compassion mixed with indignation. These sentiments occupy the mind much more than that salutary terror which the laws endeavor to inspire; but in the contemplation of continued suffering, terror is the only, or a least predominant sensation. The severity of a punishment should be just sufficient to excite compassion in the spectators, as it is intended more for them than for the criminal.

A punishment, to be just, should have only that degree of severity which is sufficient to deter others. Now there is no man, who upon the least reflection, would put in competition the total and perpetual loss of his liberty, with the greatest advantages he could possibly obtain in consequence of a crime. Perpetual slavery, then, has in it all that is necessary to deter the most hardened and determined, as much as the punishment of death. I say it has more. There are many who can look upon death with intrepidity and firmness; some through fanaticism, and others through vanity, which attends us even to the grave; others from a desperate resolution, either to get rid of their misery, or cease to live: but fanaticism and vanity forsake the criminal in slavery, in chains and fetters, in an iron cage; and despair seems rather the beginning than the end of their misery. The mind, by collecting itself and uniting all its force, can, for a moment, repel assailing grief; but its most vigorous efforts are insufficient to resist perpetual wretchedness.

In all nations, where death is used as a punishment, every example supposes a new crime committed. Whereas in perpetual slavery, every criminal affords a frequent and lasting example; and if it be necessary that men should often be witnesses of the power of the laws, criminals should often be put to death; but this supposes a frequency of crimes; and from hence this punishment will cease to have its effect, so that it must be useful and useless at the same time.

I shall be told, that perpetual slavery is as painful a punishment as death, and therefore as cruel. I answer, that if all the miserable moments in the life of a slave were collected into one point, it would be a more cruel punishment than any other; but these are scattered through his whole life, whilst the pain of death exerts all its force in a moment. There is also another advantage in the punishment of slavery, which is, that it is more terrible to the spectator than to the sufferer himself; for the spectator considers the sum of all his wretched moments, whilst the sufferer, by the misery of the present, is prevented from thinking of the future. All evils are increased by the imagination, and the sufferer finds resources and consolations, of which the spectators are ignorant; who judge by their own sensibility of what passes in a mind, by habit grown callous to misfortune.

Let us, for a moment, attend to the reasoning of a robber or assassin, who is deterred from violating the laws by the gibbet or the wheel. I am sensible, that to develop the sentiments of one's own heart, is an art which education only can teach: but although a villain may not be able to give a clear account of his principles, they nevertheless influence his conduct. He reasons thus:

> *What are these laws, that I am bound to respect, which make so great a difference between me and the rich man? He refuses me the farthing I ask of him, and excuses himself, by bidding me have recourse to labor with which he is unacquainted. Who made these laws? The rich and the great, who never deigned to visit the miserable hut of the poor; who have never seen him dividing a piece of mouldy bread, amidst the cries of his famished children and the tears of his wife. Let us break those ties, fatal to the greatest part of mankind, and only useful to a few indolent tyrants. Let us attack injustice at its source. I will return to my natural state of independence. I shall live free and happy on the fruits of my courage and industry. A day of pain and repentance may*

> *come, but it will be short; and for an hour of grief I shall enjoy years of pleasure and liberty. King of a small number, as determined as myself, I will correct the mistakes of fortune; and I shall see those tyrants grow pale and tremble at the sight of him, whom, with insulting pride, they would not suffer to rank with their dogs and horses.*

Religion then presents itself to the mind of this lawless villain, and promising him almost a certainty of eternal happiness upon the easy terms of repentance, contributes much to lessen the horror of the last scene of the tragedy.

But he who foresees, that he must pass a great number of years, even his whole life, in pain and slavery; a slave to those laws by which he was protected; in sight of his fellow citizens, with whom he lives in freedom and society; makes an useful comparison between those evils, the uncertainty of his success, and the shortness of the time in which he shall enjoy the fruits of his transgression. The example of those wretches continually before his eyes, make a much greater impression on him than a punishment, which, instead of correcting, makes him ore obdurate.

The punishment of death is pernicious to society, from the example of barbarity it affords. If the passions, or the necessity of war, have taught men to shed the blood of their fellow creatures, the laws, which are intended to moderate the ferocity of mankind, should not increase it by examples of barbarity, the more horrible, as this punishment is usually attended with formal pageantry. Is it not absurd, that the laws, which detest and punish homicide, should, in order to prevent murder, publicly commit murder themselves? What are the true and most useful laws? Those compacts and conditions which all would propose and observe, in those moments when private interest is silent, or combined with that of the public. What are the natural sentiments of every person concerning the punishment of death? We may read them in the contempt and indignation with which every one looks on the executioner, who is nevertheless an innocent executor of the public will; a good citizen, who contributes to the advantage of society; the instrument of the general security within, as good as soldiers are without. What then is the origin of this contradiction? Why is this sentiment of mankind indelible, to the scandal of reason? It is, that in a secret corner of the mind, in which the original impressions of nature are still preserved, men discover a sentiment which tells them, that their lives are not lawfully in the power of any one, but of that necessity only, which with its iron scepter rules the universe.

What must men think, when they see wise magistrates and grave ministers of justice, with indifference and tranquillity, dragging a criminal to death, and whilst a wretch trembles with agony, expecting the fatal stroke, the judge, who has condemned him, with the coldest insensibility, and perhaps with no small gratification from the exertion of his authority, quits his tribunal to enjoy the comforts and pleasures of life? They will say, "*Ah! those cruel formalities of justice are a cloak to tyranny, they are a secret language, a solemn veil, intended to conceal the sword by which we are sacrificed to the insatiable idol of despotism. Murder, which they would represent to us as an horrible crime, we see practiced by them without repugnance, or remorse. Let us follow their example. A violent death appeared terrible in their descriptions, but we see that it is the affair of a moment. It will be still less terrible to him, who not expecting it, escapes almost all the pain."*

Such is the fatal, though absurd reasoning of men who are disposed to commit crimes; on whom, the abuse of religion has more influence than religion itself.

If it be objected, that almost all nations in all ages have punished certain crimes with death, I answer, that the force of these examples vanishes, when opposed to truth, against which prescription is urged in vain. The history of mankind is an immense sea of errors, in which a few obscure truths may here and there be found.

But human sacrifices have also been common in almost all nations. That some societies only, either few in number, or for a very short time, abstained from the punishment of death, is rather favorable to my argument, for such is the fate of great truths, that their duration is only as a flash of lightning in the long and dark night of error. The happy time is not yet arrived, when truth, as falsehood has been hitherto, shall be the portion of the greatest number.

I am sensible that the voice of one philosopher is too weak to be heard amidst the clamors of a multitude, blindly influenced by custom; but there is a small number of sages, scattered on the face of the earth, who will echo to me from the bottom of their hearts; and if these truths should haply force their way to the thrones of princes, be it known to them, that they come attended with the secret wishes of all mankind; and tell the sovereign who deigns them a gracious reception, that his fame shall outline the glory of conquerors, and that equitable posterity will exalt his peaceful trophies above those of a Titus, an Antonius, or a Trajan.

How happy were mankind, if laws were now to be first formed; now that we see on the thrones of Europe, benevolent monarchs, friends to the virtues of peace, to the arts and sciences, fathers of their people, though crowned yet citizens; the increase of whose authority augments the happiness of their subjects, by destroying the intermediate despotism, which intercepts the prayers of the people, to the throne. If these human princes have suffered the old laws to subsist, it is doubtless because they are deterred by the numberless obstacles, which oppose the subversion of errors established by the sanction of many ages; and therefore every wise citizen will wish for the increase of their authority.

Chapter 29

Of Imprisonment

That a magistrate, the executor of the laws, should have a power to imprison a citizen, to deprive the man he hates of his liberty upon frivolous pretenses, and to leave his friend unpunished, notwithstanding the strongest proofs of his guilt, is an error, as common, as it is contrary to the end of society, which is personal security.

Imprisonment is a punishment, which differs from all others in this particular, that it necessarily precedes conviction; but this difference does not destroy a circumstance, which is essential and common to it with all other punishments, *viz.* that it should never be inflicted, but when ordained by the law. The law should therefore determine the crime, the presumption, and the evidence sufficient to subject the accused to imprisonment and examination. Public report, his flight, his extrajudicial confession, that of an accomplice, menaces, and his constant enmity with the person injured, the circumstances of the crime, and such other evidence, may be sufficient to justify the imprisonment of a citizen. But the nature of this evidence should be determined by the laws, and not by the magistrates, whose decrees are always contrary to political liberty, when they are not particular applications of a general maxim of the public code. When punishments become less severe, and prisons less horrible; when compassion and humanity shall penetrate the iron gates of dungeons, and direct the obdurate and inexorable ministers of justice, the laws may then be satisfied with weaker evidence for imprisonment.

A person accused, imprisoned, tried, and acquitted, ought not to be branded with any degree of infamy. Among the Romans, we see that many, accused of very great crimes and afterwards declared innocent, were respected by the people, and honored with employment in the state. But why is the fate of an innocent person so different in this age? It is, because the present system of penal laws presents to our minds an idea of power rather than of justice. It is, because the accused and convicted are thrown indiscriminately into the same prison; because imprisonment is rather a punishment, than a means of securing the person of the accused; and because the interior power, which defends the laws, and the exterior, which defends the throne and kingdom, are separate, when they should be united. If the first were (under the common authority of the laws) combined with the right of judging, but not however immediately dependent on the magistrate, the pomp that attends a military corps, would take off the infamy; which, like all popular opinions, is more attached to the manner and form, than to the thing itself; as may be seen in military imprisonment, which, in the common opinion, is not so disgraceful as the civil. But the barbarity and ferocity of our ancestors, the hunters of the North, still subsist among the people, in our customs and our laws, which are always several ages behind the actual refinements of a nation.

Chapter 30

Of Prosecution and Prescription

The proofs of the crime being obtained, and the certainty of it determined, it is necessary to allow the criminal time and means for his justification; but a time so short, as not to diminish that promptitude of punishment, which, as we have shown, is one of the most powerful means of preventing crimes. A mistaken humanity may object to the shortness of the time, but the force of the objection will vanish, if we consider that the danger of the innocent increases with the defects of the legislation.

The time for inquiry and for justification should be fixed by the laws, and not by the judge, who, in that case, would become legislator. With regard to atrocious crimes, which are long remembered, when they are once proved, if the criminal have fled, no time should be allowed; but in less considerable and more obscure crimes, a time should be fixed, after which the delinquent should be no longer uncertain of his fate. For in the latter case, the length of time, in which the crime is almost forgotten, prevents the example of impunity, and allows the criminal to amend, and become a better member of society.

General principles will here be sufficient, it being impossible to fix precisely the limits of time for any given legislation, or for any society in any particular circumstance. I shall only add, that in a nation willing to prove the utility of moderate punishment, laws, which, according to the nature of the crime, increase or diminish the time of inquiry and justification, considering the imprisonment or the voluntary exile of the criminal as a part of the punishment, will form an easy division of a small number of mild punishments for a great number of crimes.

But, it must be observed, the time for inquiry and justification should not increase in direct proportion to the atrociousness of crimes; for the probability of such crimes having been committed, is inversely as their atrociousness. Therefore the time for inquiry, ought in some cases to be diminished, and that for justification increased, *and vice versa*. This may appear to contradict what I have said above, namely, that equal punishments may be decreed for unequal crimes, by considering the time allowed the criminal, or the prison as a punishment.

In order to explain this idea, I shall divide crimes into two classes. The first comprehends homicide, and all greater crimes; the second, crimes of an inferior degree. This distinction is founded in human nature. The preservation of life is a natural right; the preservation of property is a right of society. The motives that induce men to shake off the natural sentiment of compassion, which must be destroyed before great crimes can be committed, are much less in number than those, by which, from the natural desire of being happy, they are instigated to violate a right, which is not founded in the heart of man, but is the work of society. The different degrees of probability in these two classes, requires that they should be regulated on different principles. In the greatest crimes, as they are less frequent, and the probability of the innocent of the accused being greater, the time allowed him for his justification should be greater, and the time of inquiry less. For by hastening the definitive sentence, the flattering hopes of impunity are destroyed, which are more dangerous, as the crime is more atrocious. On the contrary, in crimes of less importance, the probability of the innocence being less, the time of inquiry should be greater, and that of justification less, as impunity is not so dangerous.

But this division of crimes into two classes should not be admitted, if the consequences of impunity were in proportion to the probability of the crime. It should be considered, that a person accused, whose guilt or innocence is not determined for want of proofs, may be again imprisoned for the same crime, and be subject to a new trial, if fresh evidence arises, within the time fixed.

This is in my opinion the best method of providing, at the same time, for the security and liberty of the subject, without favoring one at the expense of the other; which may easily happen, since both these blessings, the inalienable and equal patrimony of every citizen, are liable to be invaded, the one by open or disguised despotism, and the other by tumultuous and popular anarchy.

Chapter 31

Of Crimes of Difficult Proof

With the foregoing principles in view, it will appear astonishing, that reason hardly ever presided at the formation of the laws of nations; that the weakest and most equivocal evidence, and even conjectures, have been thought sufficient proof for crimes the most atrocious, (and therefore most improbable) the most obscure and chimerical; as if it were the interest of the laws and the judge not to inquire into the truth, but to prove the crime; as if there were not a greater risk of condemning an innocent person, when the probability of his guilt is less.

The generality of men want that vigor of mind, and resolution, which are as necessary for great crimes, as for great virtues; and which at the same time produce both the one and the other in those nations, which are supported by the activity of their government, and a passion for the public good. For in those which subsist by their greatness or power, or by the goodness of their laws, the passions being in a weaker degree, seem calculated rather to maintain than to improve the form of government. This naturally leads us to an important conclusion, *viz.* that great crimes do not always produce the destruction of a nation.

There are some crimes, which, though frequent in society, are of difficult proof, a circumstance admitted, as equal to the probability of the innocence of the accused. But as the frequency of these crimes in not owing to their impunity, so much as to other causes, the danger of their passing unpunished is of less importance, and therefore the time of examination, and prescription, may be equally diminished. These principles are different from those commonly received; for it is in crimes, which are proved with the greatest difficulty, such as adultery, and sodomy, that presumptions, half proofs, etc. are admitted; as if a man could be half innocent, and half guilty; that is, half punishable and half absolvable. It is in these cases that torture should exercise its cruel power on the person of the accused, the witnesses, and even his whole family, as, with unfeeling indifference, some Civilians have taught who pretend to dictate laws to nations.

Adultery is a crime, which, politically considered, owes its existence to two cause, *viz.* pernicious laws, and the powerful attraction between the sexes. This attraction is similar in many circumstances to gravity, the spring of motion in the universe. Like this, it is diminished by distance; one regulates the motions of the body, the other of the soul. But they differ in one respect; the force of gravity decreases in proportion to the obstacles that oppose it; the other gathers strength and vigor as the obstacles increase.

If I were speaking of nations guided only by the laws of nature, I would tell them, that there is a considerable difference between adultery and all other crimes. Adultery proceeds from an abuse of that necessity, which is constant and universal in human nature; a necessity anterior to the formation of society, and indeed the founder of society itself; whereas all other crimes tend to the destruction of society, and arise from momentary passions, and not from a natural necessity. It is the opinion of those, who have studied history and mankind, that this necessity is constantly in the same degree in the same climate. If this be true, useless, or rather pernicious must all laws and customs be, which tend to diminish the sum total of the effects of this passion. Such laws would only burden one part of society with the additional necessities of the other; but, on the contrary, wise are the laws, which, following the natural course of the river, divide the stream into a number of equal branches, preventing thus both sterility and inundation.

Conjugal fidelity is always greater in proportion as marriages are more numerous, and less difficulty. But when the interest or pride of families, or paternal authority, not the inclination of the parties, unite the sexes, gallantry soon breaks the slender ties, in spite of common moralists, who exclaim against the effect, whilst they pardon the cause. But these reflections are useless to those, who, living in the true religion, act from sublimer motives, which correct the eternal laws of nature.

The act of adultery is a crime so instantaneous, so mysterious, and so concealed by the veil which the laws themselves have woven; a veil necessary indeed, but so transparent, as to heighten rather than conceal the charms of the object; the opportunities are so frequent, and the danger of discovery so easily avoided, that it were much easier for the laws to prevent this crime, than to punish it when committed.

To every crime, which, from its nature must frequently remain unpunished, the punishment is an incentive. Such is the nature of the human mind, that difficulties, if not insurmountable, not too great for our natural indolence, embellish the object, and spur us on to the pursuit. They are so many barriers that confine the imagination to the object, and oblige us to consider it in every point of view. In this agitation, the mind naturally inclines and fixes itself to the most agreeable part, studiously avoiding every idea that might create disgust.

The crime of sodomy, so severely punished by the laws, and for the proof of which are employed tortures, which often triumph over innocence itself, has its source much less in the passions of man in a free and independent state, than in society and a slave. It is much less the effect of a satiety in pleasures, than of that education, which, in order to make men useful to others, begins by making them useless to themselves. In those public seminaries, where youth are carefully excluded from all commerce with the other sex, as the vigor of nature blooms, it is consumed in a manner not only useless to mankind, but which accelerates the approach of old age.

The murder of bastard-children is, in like manner, the effect of a cruel dilemma, in which a woman finds herself who has been seduced through weakness, or overcome by force. The alternative is, either her own infamy, or the death of a being, who is incapable of feeling the loss of life. How can she avoid preferring the last to the inevitable misery of herself and her unhappy infant? The best method of preventing this crime, would be effectually to protect the weak woman from that tyranny, which exaggerates all vices that cannot be concealed under the cloak of virtue.

I do not pretend to lessen that just abhorrence which these crimes deserve, but to discover the sources from whence they spring; and I think I may draw the following conclusion:

> *That the punishment of a crime cannot be just, (that is necessary) if the laws have not endeavored to prevent that crime by the best means which times and circumstances would allow.*

Chapter 32

Of Suicide

Suicide is a crime which seems not to admit of punishment, properly speaking; for it cannot be inflicted but on the innocent, or upon an insensible dead body. In the first case, it is unjust and tyrannical, for political liberty supposes all punishments entirely personal; in the second, it has the same effect, by way of example, as the scourging a statue. Mankind love life too well; the objects that surround them; the seducing phantom of pleasure and hope, that sweetest error of mortals, which makes men swallow such large draughts of evil, mingled with a very few drops of good, allure them too strongly, to apprehend that this crime will ever be common from its unavoidable impunity. The laws are obeyed through fear of punishment, but death destroys all sensibility. What motive then can restrain the desperate hand of suicide?

He who kills himself does a less injury to society, than he who quits his country for ever; for the other leaves his property behind him, but this carries with him at least a part of his substance. Besides, as the strength of a society consists in the number of citizens, he who quits one nation to reside in another, becomes a double loss. This then is the question: whether it be advantageous to society, that its members should enjoy the unlimited privilege of migration?

Every law that is not armed with force, or which, from circumstances, must be ineffectual, should not be promulgated. Opinion, which reigns over the minds of men, obeys the slow and indirect impressions of the legislator, but resists them when violently and directly applied; and useless laws communicate their insignificance to the most salutary, which are regarded more as obstacles to be surmounted, than as safeguards of the public good. But further, our perceptions being limited, by enforcing the observance of laws which are evidently useless, we destroy the influence of the most salutary.

From this principle a wise dispenser of public happiness may draw some useful consequences, the explanation of which would carry me too far from my subject, which is to prove the inutility of making the nation a prison. Such a law is vain, because unless inaccessible rocks, or impassable seas, divide the country from all others, how will it be possible to secure every point of the circumference, or how will you guard the guards themselves? Besides, this crime once committed, cannot be punished; and to punish it beforehand, would be to punish the intention and not the action; the will, which is entirely out of the power of human laws. To punish the absent by confiscating his effects, besides the facility of collusion which would inevitably be the case, and which, without tyranny, could not be prevented, would put a stop to all commerce with other nations. To punish the criminal when he returns, would be to prevent him from repairing the evil he had already done to society, by making his absence perpetual. Besides, any prohibition would increase the desire of removing, and would infallibly prevent strangers from settling in the country.

What must we think of a government which has no means, but fear, to keep its subjects in their own country; to which, by the first impressions of their infancy, they are so strongly attached. The most certain method of keeping men at home, is, to make them happy; and it is the interest of every state to turn the balance, not only of commerce, but of felicity in favor of its subjects. The pleasures of luxury are not the principal sources of this happiness; though, by preventing the too great accumulation of wealth in a few hands, they become a necessary remedy against the too great inequality of individuals, which always increases with the progress of society.

When the populousness of a country does not increase in proportion to its extent, luxury favors despotism, for where men are most dispersed, there is least industry; and where there is least industry, the dependence of the poor upon the luxury of the rich is greatest, and the union of the oppressed against the oppressors is least to be feared. In such circumstances, rich and powerful men more easily command distinction, respect and service, by which they are raised to a greater height above the poor; for men are more independent the less they are observed, and are least observed when most numerous. On the contrary, when the number of people is too great in proportion to the extent of a country, luxury is a check to despotism; because it is a spur to industry, and because the labor of the poor affords so many pleasures to the rich, that they disregard the luxury of ostentation, which would remind the people of their dependence. Hence we see, that in vast and depopulated states, the luxury of ostentation prevails over that of convenience; but in countries more populous, the luxury of convenience tends constantly to diminish the luxury of ostentation.

The pleasures of luxury have this inconvenience, that though they employ a great number of hands, yet they are only enjoyed by a few, whilst the rest, who do not partake of them, feel the want more sensibly, on comparing their state with that of others. Security and liberty, restrained by the laws, are the basis of happiness, and when attended by these, the pleasures of luxury favor population, without which they become the instruments of tyranny. As the most noble and generous animals fly to solitude and inaccessible deserts, and abandon the fertile plains to man, their greatest enemy; so men reject pleasure itself, when offered by the hand of tyranny.

But to return. If it be demonstrated, that the laws which imprison men in their own country are vain and unjust, it will be equally true of those which punish suicide, for that can only be punished after death; which is in the power of God alone; but it is no crime, with regard to man, because the punishment falls on an innocent family. If it be objected, that the consideration of such a punishment may prevent the crime; I answer, that he who can calmly renounce the pleasure of existence; who is so weary of life, as to brave the idea of eternal misery, will never be influenced by the more distant, and less powerful considerations of family, and children.

Chapter 33

Of Smuggling

Smuggling is a real offense against the sovereign and the nation; but the punishment should not brand the offender with infamy, because this crime is not infamous in the public opinion. By inflicting infamous punishments, for crimes that are not reputed so, we destroy that idea where it may be useful. If the same punishment be decreed for killing a pheasant as for killing a man, or for forgery, all difference between those crimes will shortly vanish. It is thus that moral sentiments are destroyed in the heart of man; sentiments, the work of many ages and of much bloodshed; sentiments that are so slowly, and with so much difficulty produced, and for the establishment of which such sublime motives, and such an apparatus of ceremonies were thought necessary.

This crime is owing to the laws themselves; for the higher the duties, the greater is the advantage, and consequently, the temptation; which temptation is increased by the facility of perpetration, when the circumference that is guarded is of great extent, and the merchandise prohibited is small in bulk. The seizure and loss of the goods attempted to be smuggled, together with those that are found along with them, is just; but it would be better to lessen the duty, because men risque only in proportion to the advantage expected.

This crime being a theft of what belongs to the prince, and consequently, to the nation, why is it not attended with infamy? I answer, that crimes, which men consider as productive of no bad consequences to themselves, do not interest them sufficiently to excite their indignation. The generality of mankind, upon whom remote consequences make no impression, do not see the evil that may result from the practice of smuggling, especially if they reap from it any present advantage. They only perceive the loss sustained by the prince. They are not then interested in refusing their esteem to the smuggler, as to one who has committed a theft or a forgery, or other crimes, by which they themselves may suffer; from this evident principle, that a sensible being only interests himself in those evils, with which he is acquainted. Shall this crime then, committed by one who has nothing to lose, go unpunished? No. there are certain species of smuggling, which so particularly affect the revenue, a part of government so essential, and managed with so much difficulty, that they deserve imprisonment, or even slavery; but yet of such a nature as to be proportioned to the crime. For example, it would be highly unjust that a smuggler of tobacco should suffer the same punishment with a robber, or assassin; but it would be most conformable to the nature of the offense, that the produce of his labor should be applied to the use of the crown, which he intended to defraud.

Chapter 34

Of Bankrupts

The necessity of good faith in contrasts, and the support of commerce, oblige the legislature to secure for the creditors, the persons of bankrupts. It is, however, necessary to distinguish between the fraudulent and the honest bankrupt. The fraudulent bankrupt should be punished in the same manner with him who adulterates the coin; for to falsify a piece of coin, which is a pledge of the mutual obligations between citizens, is not a greater crime than to violate the obligations themselves. But the bankrupt who, after a strict examination, has proved before proper judges, that either the fraud, or losses of others, or misfortunes unavoidable by human prudence, have stripped him of his substance; upon what barbarous pretence is he thrown into prison, and thus deprived of the only remaining good, the melancholy enjoyment of mere liberty? Why is he ranked with criminals, and in despair compelled to repent of his honesty? Conscious of his innocence, he lived easy and happy under the protection of those laws, which, it is true, he violated but not intentionally. Laws, dictated by the avarice of the rich, and accepted by the poor, seduced by the universal and flattering hope which makes men believe, that all unlucky accidents are the lot of others, and the most fortunate only their share. Mankind, when influenced by the first impressions, love cruel laws, although, being subject to them themselves, it is the interest of every person that they should be as mild as possible; but the fear of being injured is always more prevalent than the intention of injuring others.

But to return to the honest bankrupt. Let his debt, if you will, not be considered as canceled, 'till the payment of the whole; let him be refused the liberty of leaving the country without leave of his creditors, or of carrying into another nation that industry, which, under a penalty, be should be obliged to employ for their benefit; but what pretence can justify the depriving an innocent, though unfortunate man of his liberty, without the least utility to his creditors?

But say they, the hardships of consignment will induce him to discover his fraudulent transactions; an event, that can hardly be supposed, after a rigorous examination of his conduct and affairs. But if they are not discovered, he will escape unpunished. It is, I think, a maxim of government, that the importance of the political inconveniences, arising from the impunity of a crime, are directly as the injury to the public, and inversely as the difficulty of proof.

It will be necessary to distinguish fraud attended with aggravating circumstances from simple fraud, and that from perfect innocence. For the first, let there be ordained the same punishment as for forgery; for the second, a less punishment, but with the loss of liberty; and if perfectly honest, let the bankrupt himself choose the method of re-establishing himself and of satisfying his creditors; or if he should appear not to have been strictly honest, let that be determined by his creditors. But these distinctions should be fixed by the laws, which alone are impartial, and not by the arbitrary and dangerous prudence of Judges.

It may be alleged, that the interest of commerce and property should be secured; but commerce and property are not the end of the social compact, but the means of obtaining that end; and to expose all the members of society to cruel laws, to preserve them from evils, necessarily occasioned by the infinite combinations which result from the actual state of political societies, would be to make the end subservient to the means, a paralogism in all sciences, and particularly in politics. In the former editions of this work, I myself fell into this error, when I said that the honest bankrupt should be kept in custody, as a pledge for his debts, or employed, as a slave, to work for his creditors. I am ashamed of having adopted so cruel an opinion. I have been accused of impiety; I did not deserve it. I have been accused of sedition; I deserved as little. But I insulted all the rights of humanity, and was never reproached.

With what ease might a sagacious legislator prevent the greatest part of fraudulent bankruptcies, and remedy the misfortunes that befall the honest and industrious! A public register of all contracts, with the liberty of consulting it allowed to every citizen; a public fund formed by a contribution of the opulent merchants for the timely assistance of unfortunate industry, were establishments that could produce no real inconveniences, and many advantages. But unhappily, the most simple, the easiest, yet the wisest laws, that wait only for the nod of the legislator, to diffuse through nations, wealth, power, and felicity; laws, which would be regarded by future generations with eternal gratitude, are either unknown, or rejected. A restless, and trifling spirit, the timid prudence of the present moment, a distrust and aversion to the most useful novelties, possess the minds of those who are empowered to regulate the actions of mankind.

Chapter 35

Of Sanctuaries

Are sanctuaries just? Is a convention between nations mutually to give up their criminals, useful?

In the whole extent of a political state, there should be no place independent of the laws. Their power should follow every subject, as the shadow follows the body. Sanctuaries and impunity differ only in degree, and as the effect of punishments depends more on their certainty, than their greatness, men are more strongly invited to crimes by sanctuaries, than they are deterred by punishment. To increase the number of sanctuaries, is to erect so many little sovereignties; for, where the laws have no power, new bodies will be formed in opposition to the public good, and a spirit established contrary to that of the state. History informs us, that from the use of sanctuaries have arisen the greatest revolutions in kingdoms, and in opinions.

Some have pretended, that in whatever country a crime, that is an action contrary to the laws of society, be committed, the criminal may be justly punished for it in any other: as if the character of subject were indelible, or synonymous with, or worse than that of slave; as if a man could live in one country, and be subject to the laws of another, or be accountable for his actions to two sovereigns, or two codes of laws, often contradictory. There are also who think, that an act of cruelty committed, for example, at Constantinople, may be punished at Paris; for this abstracted reason, that he who offends humanity, should have enemies in all mankind, and be the object of universal execration; as if judges were to be the knights errant of human nature in general, rather than guardians of particular conventions between men. The place of punishment can certainly be no other, than that where the crime was committed; for the necessity of punishing an individual for the general good subsists there, and there only. A villain, if he has not broke through the conventions of a society, of which by my supposition he was not a member, may be feared, and by force banished and excluded from that society; but ought not to be formally punished by the laws, which were only intended to maintain the social compact, and not to punish the intrinsic malignity of actions.

Whether it be useful that nations should mutually deliver up their criminals? Although the certainty of there being no part of the earth where crimes are not punished, may be a means of preventing them, I shall not pretend to determine this question, until laws more conformable to the necessities and rights of humanity, and until milder punishments, and the abolition of the arbitrary power of opinion, shall afford security to virtue and innocence when oppressed; and until tyranny shall be confined to the plains of Asia, and Europe acknowledge the universal empire of reason, by which the interests of sovereigns, and subjects, are best united.

Chapter 36

Of Rewards for Apprehending, or Killing Criminals

Let us inquire, whether it be advantageous to society, to set a price on the head of a criminal, and so to make of every citizen an executioner. If the offender hath taken refuge in another state, the sovereign encourages his subjects to commit a crime, and to expose themselves to a just punishment; he insults that nation, and authorizes the subjects to commit on their similar usurpations. If the criminal still remain in his own country, to set a price upon his head, is the strongest proof of the weakness of the government. He who has strength to defend himself, will not purchase the assistance of another. Besides such an edict confounds all the ideas of virtue, and morality, already too wavering in the mind of man. At one time treachery is punished by the laws, at another encouraged. With one hand the legislature strengthens the ties of kindred, and friendship, and with the other, rewards the violation of both. Always in contradiction with himself, now he invites the suspecting minds of men to mutual confidence, and now he plants distrust in every heart. To prevent one crime, he gives birth to a thousand. Such are the expedients of weak nations, whose laws are like temporary repairs to a tottering fabric. On the contrary, as a nation becomes more enlightened, honesty and mutual confidence become more necessary, and are daily tending to unite with sound policy. Artifice, cabal, and obscure and indirect actions are more easily discovered, and the interest of the whole is better secured against the passions of the individual.

Even the times of ignorance, when private virtue was encouraged by public morality, may afford instruction and example to more enlightened ages. But laws, which reward treason, excite clandestine war, and mutual distrust, and oppose that necessary union of morality and policy, which is the foundation of happiness, and universal peace.

Chapter 37

Of Attempts, Accomplices, and Pardons

The laws do not punish the intention; nevertheless, an attempt, which manifests the intention of committing a crime, deserves a punishment; though less, perhaps, than if the crime were actually perpetrated. The importance of preventing even attempts to commit a crime sufficiently authorizes a punishment; but as there may be an interval of time between the attempt and the execution, it is proper to reserve the greater punishment for the actual commission, that even after the attempt there may be a motive for desisting.

In like manner, with regard to the accomplices, they ought not to suffer so severe a punishment as the immediate perpetrator of the crime. But this for a different reason. When a number of men unite, and run a common risk, the greater the danger, the more they endeavor to distribute it equally. Now, if the principals be punished more severely than the accessories, it will prevent the danger from being equally divided, and will increase the difficulty of finding a person to execute the crime, as his danger is greater by the difference of the punishment. There can be but one exception to this rule; and that is, when the principal receives a reward from the accomplices. In that case, as the difference of the danger is compensated, the punishment should be equal.

These reflections may appear too refined to those who do not consider, that it is of great importance, that the laws should leave the associates as few means as possible of agreeing among themselves.

In some tribunals a pardon is offered to an accomplice in a great crime, if he discover his associates. This expedient has its advantages and disadvantages. The disadvantages are, that the law authorizes treachery, which is detested even by the villains themselves; and introduces crimes of cowardice, which are much more pernicious to a nation than crimes of courage. Courage is not common, and only wants a benevolent power to direct it to the public good. Cowardice, on the contrary, is a frequent, self-interested and contagious evil, which can never be improved into a virtue. Besides, the tribunal, which has recourse to this method, betrays its fallibility, and the laws their weakness, by imploring the assistance of those by whom they are violated.

The advantages are, that it prevents great crimes, the effects of which being public, and the perpetrators concealed, terrify the people. It also contributes to prove, that he who violates the laws, which are public conventions, will also violate private compacts. It appears to me, that a general law, promising a reward to every accomplice who discovers his associates, would be better than a special declaration in every particular case; because it would prevent the union of those villains, as it would inspire a mutual distrust, and each would be afraid of exposing himself alone to danger. The accomplice, however, should be pardoned, on condition of transportation.... But it is in vain, that I torment myself with endeavoring to extinguish the remorse I feel in attempting to induce the sacred laws, the monument of public confidence, the foundation of human morality, to authorize dissimulation and perfidy. But what an example does it offer to a nation, to see the interpreters of the laws break their promise of pardon, and on the strength of learned subtleties, and to the scandal of public faith, drag him to punishment who hath accepted of their invitation! Such examples are not uncommon, and this is the reason, that political society is regarded as a complex machine, the springs of which are moved at pleasure by the most dexterous or most powerful.

Chapter 38

Of Suggestive Interrogations

The laws forbid *suggestive interrogations*; that is, according to the civilians, questions, which, with regard to the circumstances of the crime, are *special* when they should be *general*; or, in other words, those questions, which having an immediate reference to the crime, suggest to the criminal an immediate answer. Interrogations, according to the law, ought to lead to the fact indirectly and obliquely, but never directly or immediately. The intent of this injunction is either, that they should not suggest to the accused an immediate answer that might acquit him, or that they think it contrary to nature that a man should accuse himself. But whatever be the motive, the laws have fallen into a palpable contradiction, in condemning suggestive interrogations, whilst they authorize torture. Can there be an interrogation more suggestive than pain? Torture will suggest to a robust villain an obstinate silence, that he may exchange a greater punishment for a less; and to a feeble man confession, to relieve him from the present pain, which affects him more than the apprehension of the future. If a special interrogation be contrary to the right of nature, as it obliges a man to accuse himself, torture will certainly do it more effectually. But men are influenced more by the names than the nature of things.

He, who obstinately refuses to answer the interrogative, deserves a punishment, which should be fixed by the laws, and that of the severest kind; that criminals should not, by their silence, evade the example which they owe the public. But this punishment is not necessary when the guilt of the criminal is indisputable, because in that case interrogation is useless, as is likewise his confession, when there are, without it, proofs sufficient. This last case is most common, for experience shows, that in the greatest number of criminal prosecutions, the culprit pleads not guilty.

Chapter 39

Of a Particular Kind of Crime

The reader will perceive, that I have omitted speaking of a certain class of crimes which has covered Europe with blood, and raised up those horrid piles, from whence, midst clouds of whirling smoke, the groans of human victims, the crackling of their bones, and the frying of their still panting bowels, were a pleasing spectacle, and agreeable harmony to the fanatic multitude. But men of understanding will perceive, that the age and country, in which I live, will not permit me to inquire into the nature of this crime. It were too tedious, and foreign to my subject, to prove the necessity of a perfect uniformity of opinions, in a state, contrary to the examples of many nations; to prove that opinions, which differ from one another only in some subtle and obscure distinctions, beyond the reach of human capacity, may nevertheless disturb the public tranquillity, unless one only religion be established by authority; and that some opinions, by being contrasted and opposed to each other, in their collision strike out the truth; whilst others, feeble in themselves, require the support of power and authority. It should, I say, carry me too far, were I to prove, that how odious soever is the empire of force over the opinions of mankind, from whom it only obtains dissimulation, followed by contempt; and, although it may seem contrary to the spirit of humanity and brotherly love, commanded us by reason, and authority, which we more respect, it is nevertheless necessary and indispensable. We are to believe, that all these paradoxes are solved beyond a doubt, and are conformable to the true interests of mankind, if practiced by a lawful authority. I write only of *crimes* which violate the laws of nature and the social contract, and not of *sins*, even the temporal punishments of which must be determined from other principles, than those of limited human philosophy.

Chapter 40

Of False Ideas of Utility

A principal source of errors and injustice, are false ideas of utility. For example, that legislator has false ideas of utility, who considers particular more than general conveniences; who had rather command the sentiments of mankind, than excite them, and dares say to reason, "Be thou a slave;" who would sacrifice a thousand real advantages, to the fear of an imaginary or trifling inconvenience; who would deprive men of the use of fire, for fear of their being burnt, and of water, for fear of their being drowned; and who knows of no means of preventing evil but by destroying it.

The laws of this nature, are those which forbid to wear arms, disarming those only who are not disposed to commit the crime which the laws mean to prevent. Can it be supposed, that those who have the courage to violate the most sacred laws of humanity, and the most important of the code, will respect the less considerable and arbitrary injunctions, the violation of which is so easy, and of so little comparative importance? Does not the execution of this law deprive the subject of that personal liberty, so dear to mankind and to the wise legislator; and does it not subject the innocent to all the disagreeable circumstances that should only fall on the guilty? It certainly makes the situation of the assaulted worse, and of the assailants better, and rather encourages than prevents murder, as it requires less courage to attack armed than unarmed persons.

It is a false idea of utility, that would give to a multitude of sensible beings, that symmetry and order, which inanimate matter is alone capable of receiving; to neglect the present, which are the only motives that act with force and constancy on the multitude, for the more distant, whose impressions are weak and transitory, unless increased by that strength of imagination, so very uncommon among mankind. Finally, that it is a false idea of utility, which, sacrificing things to names, separates the public good from that of individuals.

There is this difference between a state of society and a state of nature, that a savage does no more mischief to another than is necessary to procure some benefit to himself; but a man in society is sometimes tempted, from a fault in the laws, to injure another, without any prospect of advantage. The tyrant inspires his vassals with fear and servility, which rebound upon him with double force, and are the cause of his torment. Fear, the more private and domestic it is, the less dangerous is it to him who makes it the instrument of his happiness; but the more it is public, and the greater number of people it affects, the greater is the probability that some mad, desperate, or designing person will seduce others to his party, by flattering expectations; and this will be the more easily accomplished, as the danger of the enterprise will be divided amongst a greater number, because the value the unhappy set upon their existence is less as their misery is greater.

Chapter 41

Of the Means of Preventing Crimes

It is better to prevent crimes, than to punish them. This is the fundamental principle of good legislation, which is the art of conducting men to the *maximum* of happiness, and to the *minimum* of misery, if we may apply this mathematical expression to the good and evil of life. But the means hitherto employed for that purpose, are generally inadequate, or contrary to the end proposed. It is impossible to reduce the tumultuous activity of mankind to absolute regularity; for, midst the various and opposite attractions of pleasure and pain, human laws are not sufficient entirely to prevent disorders in society. Such however is the chimera of weak men, when invested with authority. To prohibit a number of indifferent actions, is not to prevent the crimes which they may produce, but to create new ones; it is to change at will the ideas of virtue and vice, which, at other times, we are told are eternal and immutable. To what a situation should we be reduced, if every thing were to be forbidden that might possibly lead to a crime? We must be deprived of the use of our senses. For one motive that induces a man to commit a real crime, there are a thousand which excite him to those indifferent actions, which are called crimes by bad laws. If, then, the probability that a crime will be committed, be in proportion to the number of motives, to extend the sphere of crimes will be to increase that probability. The generality of laws are only exclusive privileges; the tribute of all to the advantage of a few.

Would you prevent crimes? Let the laws be clear and simple; let the entire force of the nation be united in their defense; let them be intended rather to savor every individual, than any particular classes of men; let the laws be feared, and the laws only. The fear of the laws is salutary, but the fear of men is a fruitful and fatal source of crimes. Men enslaved, are more voluptuous, more debauched, and more cruel than those who are in a state of freedom. These study the sciences, the interest of nations, have great objects before their eyes, and imitate them; but those, whose views are confined to the present moment, endeavor, midst the distraction of riot, and debauchery, to forget their situation; accustomed to the uncertainty of all events, for the laws determine none, the consequences of their crimes become problematical, which gives an additional force to the strength of their passions.

In a nation, indolent from the nature of the climate, the uncertainty of the laws confirms and increases men's indolence and stupidity. In a voluptuous, but active nation, this uncertainty occasions a multiplicity of cabals and intrigues, which spread distrust and diffidence through the hearts of all, and dissimulation and treachery are the foundation of their prudence. In a brave and powerful nation, this uncertainty of the laws is at last destroyed, after many oscillations from liberty to slavery, and from slavery to liberty again.

Chapter 42

Of the Sciences

Would you prevent crimes? Let liberty be attended with knowledge. As knowledge extends, the disadvantages which attend it diminish, and the advantages increase. A daring impostor, who is always a man of some genius, is adored by the ignorant populace, and despised by men of understanding. Knowledge facilitates the comparison of objects, by showing them in different points of view. When the clouds of ignorance are dispelled by the radiance of knowledge, authority trembles, but the force of the laws remains immovable. Men of enlightened understanding must necessarily approve those useful conventions, which are the foundation of public safety; they compare, with the highest satisfaction, the inconsiderable portion of liberty of which they are deprived, with the sum total sacrificed by others for their security; observing that they have only given up the pernicious liberty of injuring their fellow creatures, they bless the throne, and the laws upon which it is established.

It is false that the sciences have always been prejudicial to mankind. When they were so, the evil was inevitable. The multiplication of the human species on the face of the earth introduced war, the rudiments of arts, and the first laws, which were temporary compacts arising from necessity, and perishing with it. This was the first philosophy, and its few elements were just, as indolence and want of sagacity, in the early inhabitants of the world, preserved them from error.

But necessities increasing with the number of mankind, stronger and more lasting impressions were necessary to prevent their frequent relapses into a state of barbarity, which became every day more fatal. The first religious errors, which peopled the earth with false divinities, and created a world of invisible beings to govern the visible creation, were of the utmost service mankind. The greatest benefactors to humanity were those who dared to deceive, and lead pliant ignorance to the foot of the altar. By presenting to the minds of the vulgar, things out of the reach of their senses, which fled as they pursued, and always eluded their grasp; which, as they never comprehended, they never despised, their different passions were united, and attached to a single object. This was the first transition of all nations from their savage state. Such was the necessary, and perhaps the only bond of all societies at their first formation. I speak not of the chosen people of God, to whom the most extraordinary miracles, and the most signal favors, supplied the place of human policy. But as it is the nature of error to sub--divide itself *ad infinitum*, so the pretended knowledge, which sprung from it, transformed mankind into a blind fanatic multitude, jarring and destroying each other in the labyrinth in which they were enclosed: hence it is not wonderful, that some sensible and philosophic minds should regret the ancient state of barbarity. This was the first epoch, in which knowledge, or rather opinions, were fatal.

The second may be found in the difficult and terrible passage from error to truth, from darkness to light. The violent shock between a mass of errors, useful to the few and powerful, and the truths so important to the many and the weak, with the fermentation of passions, excited on that occasion, were productive of infinite evils to unhappy mortals. In the study of history, whose principal periods, after certain intervals, much resemble each other, we frequently find, in the necessary passage from the obscurity of ignorance to the light of philosophy, and from tyranny to liberty, its natural consequence, one generation sacrificed to the happiness of the next. But when this flame is extinguished, and the world delivered from its evils, after a very slow progress, sits down with monarchs on the throne, and is worshipped in the assemblies of nations. Shall we then believe, that light diffused among the people is more destructive than darkness, and that the knowledge of the relations of things can ever be fatal to mankind?

Ignorance may indeed be less fatal than a small degree of knowledge, because this adds, to the evils of ignorance, the inevitable errors of a confined view of things on this side the bounds of truth; but a man of enlightened understanding, appointed guardian of the laws, is the greatest blessing that a sovereign can bestow on a nation. Such a man is accustomed to behold truth, and not to fear it; unacquainted with the greatest part of those imaginary and insatiable necessities, which so often put virtue to the proof, and accustomed to contemplate mankind from the most elevated point of view, he considers the nation as his family, and his fellow citizens as brothers; the distance between the great and the vulgar appears to him the less, as the number of mankind he has in view is greater.

The philosopher has necessities and interests unknown to the vulgar, and the chief of these is not to belie in public the principles he taught in obscurity, and the habit of loving virtue for its own sake. A few such philosophers would constitute the happiness of a nation; which, however, would be but of short duration, unless by good laws, the number were so increased, as to lessen the probability of an improper choice.

Chapter 43

Of Magistrates

Another method of preventing crimes is, to make the observance of the laws, and not their violation, the interest of the magistrate.

The greater the number of those who constitute the tribunal, the less is the danger of corruption; because the attempt will be more difficult, and the power and temptation of each individual will be proportionably less. If the sovereign, by pomp and the austerity of edicts, and by refusing to hear the complaints of the oppressed, accustom his subjects to respect the magistrates more than the laws, the magistrates will gain indeed, but it will be at the expense of public and private security.

Chapter 44

Of Rewards

Yet another method of preventing crimes is, to reward virtue. Upon this subject the laws of all nations are silent. If the rewards, proposed by academies for the discovery of useful truths, have increased our knowledge, and multiplied good books, is it not probable, that rewards, distributed by the beneficent hand of a sovereign, would also multiply virtuous actions. The coin of honour is inexhaustible, and is abundantly fruitful in the hands of a prince who distributes it wisely.

Chapter 45

Of Education

Finally, the most certain method of preventing crimes is, to perfect the system of education. But this is an object too vast, and exceeds my plan; an object, if I may venture to declare it, which is so intimately connected with the nature of government, that it will always remain a barren spot, cultivated only by a few wise men.

A great man, who is persecuted by that world he hath enlightened, and to whom we are indebted for many important truths, hath most amply detailed the principal maxims of useful education. This chiefly consists in presenting to the mind a small number of select objects; in substituting the originals for the copies, both of physical and moral phenomena; in leading the pupil to virtue by the easy road of sentiment, and in withholding him from evil by the infallible power of necessary inconveniences, rather than by command, which only obtains a counterfeit and momentary obedience.

Chapter 46

Of Pardons

As punishments become more mild, clemency and pardon are less necessary. Happy the nation in which they will be considered as dangerous! Clemency, which has often been deemed a sufficient substitute for every other virtue in sovereigns, should be excluded in a perfect legislation, where punishments are mild, and the proceedings in criminal cases regular and expeditious. This truth will seem cruel to those who live in countries, where, from the absurdity of the laws, and the severity of punishments, pardons, and the clemency of the prince, are necessary. It is indeed one of the noblest prerogatives of the throne, but, at the same time, a tacit disapprobation of the laws. Clemency is a virtue which belongs to the legislator, and not to the executor of the laws; a virtue which ought to shine in the code, and not in private judgment. To show mankind, that crimes are sometimes pardoned, and that punishment is not the necessary consequence, is to nourish the flattering hope of impunity, and is the cause of their considering every punishment inflicted as an act of injustice and oppression. The prince in pardoning, gives up the public security in favor of an individual, and, by his ill-judged benevolence, proclaims a public act of impunity.

Let, then, the executors of the laws be inexorable, but let the legislator be tender, indulgent and humane. He is a wise architect, who erects his edifice on the foundation of self-love, and contrives, that the interest of the public shall be the interest of each individual; who is not obliged by particular laws, and irregular proceedings, to separate the public good from that of individuals, and erect the image of public felicity on the basis of fear and distrust; but like a wise philosopher, he will permit his brethren to enjoy, in quiet, that small portion of happiness, which the immense system, established by the first cause, permits them to taste on earth, which is but a point in the universe.

A small crime is sometimes pardoned, if the person offended chooses to forgive the offender. This may be an act of good-nature and humanity, but it is contrary to the good of the public. For, although a private citizen may dispense with satisfaction for the injury he has received, he cannot remove the necessity of example. The right of punishing belongs not to any individual in particular, but to society in general, or the sovereign. He may renounce his own portion of this right, but cannot give up that of others.

Chapter 47

Conclusion

I conclude with this reflection, that the severity of punishments ought to be in proportion to the state of the nation. Among a people hardly yet emerged from barbarity, they should be most severe, as strong impressions are required; but in proportion as the minds of men become softened by their intercourse in society, the severity of punishments should be diminished, if it be intended, that the necessary relation between the object and the sensation should be maintained.

From what I have written results the following general theorem, of considerable utility, though not conformable to custom, the common legislator of nations.

That a punishment may not be an act of violence, of one, or of many against a private member of society, it should be public, immediate and necessary; the least possible in the case given; proportioned to the crime, and determined by the laws.

THE DECLARATION OF CAUSES

THE DECLARATION

As Adopted by
Congress [6 July 1775]

A Declaration by the Representatives of the United Colonies of North America, now met in Congress at Philadelphia, setting forth the Causes and Necessities of their taking up Arms.

If it were possible for Men, who exercise their Reason to believe, that the Divine Author of our Existence intended a Part of the human Race to hold an absolute Property in, and an unbounded Power over others, marked out by his infinite Goodness and Wisdom, as the Objects of a legal Domination never rightfully resistible, however severe and oppressive, the Inhabitants of these Colonies might at least require from the Parliament of Great-Britain some Evidence, that this dreadful Authority over them has been granted to that Body. But a Reverence for our great Creator, Principles of Humanity, and the Dictates of Common Sense, must convince all those who reflect upon the Subject that Government was instituted to promote the Welfare of Mankind, and ought to be administered for the Attainment of that End. The Legislature of Great-Britain, however, stimulated by an inordinate Passion for a Power not only unjustifiable, but which they know to be peculiarly reprobated by the very Constitution of that Kingdom, and desperate of Success in any Mode of Contest, where Regard should be had to Truth, Law, or Right, have at Length, deserting those, attempted to effect their cruel and impolitic Purpose of enslaving these Colonies by Violence, and have thereby rendered it necessary for us to close with their last Appeal from Reason to Arms. Yet, however blinded that Assembly may be, by their intemperate Range for unlimited Domination, so to Slight of Justice and the Opinion of Mankind, we esteem ourselves bound by Obligations of Respect to the Rest of the World, to make known the Justice of our Cause.

Our Forefathers, Inhabitants of the Island of Great-Britain, left their Native Land, to seek on these Shores a Residence for civil and religious Freedom. At the Expense of their Blood, at the Hazard of their Fortunes, without the least Charge to the Country which they removed, by unceasing Labor and an unconquerable Spirit, they effected Settlements in the distant and inhospitable Wilds of America, then filled with numerous and warlike Nations of Barbarians. Societies or Governments vested with perfect Legislatures, were formed under Charters from the Crown, and an harmonious Intercourse was established between the Colonies and the Kingdom from which they derived their Origin. The mutual Benefits of this Union became in a short Time so extraordinary, as to excite Astonishment. It is universally confessed, that the amazing Increase of the Wealth,

Strength, and Navigation of the Realm, arose from this Source; and the Minister, who so wisely and successfully directed the Measures of Great-Britain in the late War, publicly declared, that these Colonies enabled her to triumph over her Enemies. Towards the Conclusion of that War, it pleased our Sovereign to make a Change in his Counsels, From that fatal Moment, the Affairs of the British Empire began to fall into Confusion, and gradually sliding from the Summit of glorious Prosperity to which they had been advanced by the Virtues and Abilities of one Man, are at length distracted by the Convulsions, that now shake it to its deepest Foundations. The new Ministry finding the brave Foes of Britain, though frequently defeated, yet still contending, took up the unfortunate Idea of granting them a hasty Peace, and of then subduing her faithful Friends.

These devoted Colonies were judged to be in such a State, as to present Victories without Bloodshed, and all the easy Emoluments of statutable Plunder. The uninterrupted Tenor of their peaceable and respectful Behavior from the Beginning of Colonization, their dutiful, zealous, and useful Services during the War, though so recently and amply acknowledged in the most honorable Manner by his Majesty, by the late King, and by Parliament, could not save them from the meditated Innovations. Parliament was influenced to adopt the pernicious Project, and assuming a new Power over them, have in the course of eleven years given such decisive Specimens of the Spirit and Consequences attending this Power, as to leave no Doubt concerning the Effects of Acquiescence under it. They have undertaken to give and grant our Money without our Consent, though we have ever exercised and exclusive Right to dispose of our own Property; Statutes have been passed for extending the Jurisdiction of Courts of Admiralty and Vice-Admiralty beyond their ancient Limits; for depriving us of the accustomed and inestimable Privilege of Trial by Jury in Cases effecting both Life and Property; for suspending the Legislature of one of the Colonies; for interdicting all Commerce to the Capital of another; and for altering fundamentally the Form of Government established by Charter, and secured by Acts of its own Legislature solemnly confirmed by the Crown; for exempting the "Murderers" of Colonists from legal Trial, and in Effect, from Punishment; for erecting in a neighboring Province, acquired by the joint Arms of Great Britain and America, a Despotism dangerous to our very Existence; and for quartering Soldiers upon the Colonists in time of profound Peace. It has also been resolved in Parliament, that Colonists charged with committing certain Offenses, shall be transported to England to be tried.

But why should we enumerate our Injuries in detail? By one Statute it is declared, that Parliament can "of right make Laws to bind us in all Cases whatsoever." What is to defend us against so enormous, so unlimited a Power? Not a single Man of those who assume it, is chosen by us; or is subject to our Control or Influence; but on the Contrary, they are all of them exempt from the Operation of such Laws, and an American Revenue, if not diverted from the ostensible Purpose for which it is raised, would actually lighten their own burdens in Proportion, as they increase ours. We saw the Misery to which such Despotism would reduce us. We for Years incessantly and ineffectually besiege the Throne as Supplicants; we reasoned, we remonstrated with parliament in the most mild and decent Language. Administration sensible that we should regard these oppressive Measures as Freemen ought to do, sent over Fleets and Armies to enforce them. The Indignation of the Americans was roused, it is true; but it was the Indignation of a virtuous, loyal and affectionate People. A Congress of Delegates from the United Colonies was assembled at Philadelphia, on the fifth Day of last September. We resolve to offer an humble and dutiful Petition to the King, and also addressed our Fellow Subjects of Great-Britain. We have pursued every temperate, every respectful Measure; we have even proceeded to break off our Commercial Intercourse with our Fellow Subjects, as the last peaceable Admonition, that our Attachment to no Nation upon Earth should supplant our Attachment to Liberty. This, we flattered ourselves, was the ultimate Step of the Controversy: But subsequent Events have shown, how vain was this Hope of finding Moderation in our Enemies.

Several threatening Expressions against the Colonies were inserted in His Majesty's Speech; our Petition, tho' we were told it was a Decent one, and that his Majesty had been pleased to receive it graciously, and to promise laying it before his Parliament, was huddled into both Houses among a Bundle of American Papers, and there neglected. The Lords and Commons in their Address, in the Month of February, said, that "a Rebellion at that Time actually existed within the Province of Massachusetts-Bay; and that those concerned in it, had been countenanced and encouraged by unlawful Combinations and Engagements, entered into by his Majesty's Subjects in several of the other colonies; and therefore they besought his Majesty, that he would take the most effectual Measures to enforce due Obedience to the Laws and Authority of the Supreme Legislature." Soon after, the commercial Intercourse of whole Colonies, with foreign Countries, and with each other, was cut off by an Act of Parliament; by another, several of them were entirely prohibited from the Fisheries in the Seas near their Coasts, on which they always depended for their Sustenance; and large Re-enforcements of Ships and Troops were immediately sent over to General Gage.

Fruitless were all the entreaties, arguments, and eloquence of an Illustrious Band of the most distinguished Peers, and Commoners, who nobly and strenuously asserted the Justice of our Cause, to stay, or even to migrate the heedless fury with which these accumulated and unexampled Outrages were hurried on. Equally fruitless was the interference of the City of London, of Bristol, and many other respectable Towns in our Favor. Parliament adopted an insidious Manoeuvre calculated to divide us, to establish a perpetual Auction of Taxation where Colony should bid against Colony, all of them uninformed what Ransom would redeem their Lives; and thus to extort from us, the Point of the Bayonet, the unknown sums that should be sufficient to gratify, if possible to gratify, ministerial Rapacity, with the miserable indulgence left to us of raising, in our own Mode, the prescribed Tribute. What Terms more rigid and humiliating could have been dictated by remorseless Victors to conquered Enemies? In our circumstances to accept them, would be to deserve them.

Soon after the Intelligence of these proceedings arrived on this Continent, General Gage, who in the course of the last Year had taken possession of the Town of Boston, in the Province of Massachusetts-Bay, and still occupied it as a Garrison, on the 19th day of April, sent out from that Place a large detachment of his Army, who made an unprovoked Assault on the Inhabitants of the said Province, at the Town of Lexington, as appears by the Affidavits of a great Number of Persons, some of whom were Officers and Soldiers of that detachment, murdered eight of the Inhabitants, and wounded many others. From thence the Troops proceeded in warlike Array to the Town of Concord where they set upon by another Party of the Inhabitants of the same Province, killing several and wounding more, until compelled to retreat by the country People suddenly assembled to repel this cruel Aggression. Hostilities, thus commenced by the British Troops, have been since prosecuted by them without regard to Faith or Reputation. The Inhabitants of Boston being confined within that Town by the General their Governor, and having, in order to procure their dismission, entered into a Treaty with him, it was stipulated that the said Inhabitants having deposited their Arms with their own Magistrates, should have liberty to depart, taking with them their other Effects. They accordingly delivered up their Arms, but in open violation of Honour, in defiance of the obligation of Treaties, which even savage Nations esteemed sacred, the Governor ordered the Arms deposited as aforesaid, that they might be preserved for their owners, to be seized by a Body of Soldiers; detained the greatest part of the Inhabitants in the Town, and compelled the few who were permitted to retire, to leave their most valuable Effects behind.

By this perfidy Wives are separated from their Husbands, Children from their Parents, the aged and the sick from their Relations and Friends, who wish to attend and comfort them; and those who have been used to live in Plenty and even Elegance, are reduced to deplorable Distress.

The General, further emulating his ministerial Masters, by a Proclamation bearing date on the 12th day of June, after venting the grossest Falsehoods and Calumnies against the good People of these Colonies, proceeds to "declare them all, either by name or Description, to be Rebels and Traitors, to supersede the course of the Common Law, and instead thereof to publish and order the use and exercise of the Law Martial." His Troops have butchered our Countrymen, have wantonly burnt Charlestown, besides a considerable number of Houses in other Places; our ships and Vessels are seized; the necessary supplies of Provisions are intercepted, and he is exerting his utmost Power to spread destruction and devastation around him.

We have received certain Intelligence, that General Carleton, the Governor of Canada, is instigating the People of that Province and the Indians to fall upon us; and we have but too much reason to apprehend, that Schemes have been formed to excite domestic Enemies against us. In brief, a part of these Colonies now feel, and all of them are sure of feeling, as far as the Vengeance of Administration can inflict them, the complicated Calamities of Fire, Sword, and Famine. We are reduced to the alternative of choosing an unconditional Submission to the tyranny of irritated Ministers, or resistance by Force. The latter is our choice. We have counted the cost of this contest, and find nothing so dreadful as voluntary Slavery. Honour, Justice, and

Humanity, forbid us tamely to surrender that Freedom which we received from our gallant Ancestors, and which our innocent Posterity have a right to receive from us. We cannot endure the infamy and guilt of resigning succeeding Generations to that wretchedness which inevitably awaits them, if we basely entail hereditary Bondage upon them.

Our cause is just. Our union is perfect. Our internal Resources are great, and, if necessary, foreign Assistance is undoubtedly attainable. We gratefully acknowledge, as signal Instances of the Divine Favor towards us, that his Providence would not permit us to be called into this severe Controversy, until we were grown up to our present strength, had been previously exercised in warlike Operation, and possessed of the means of defending ourselves. With hearts fortified with these animating Reflections, we most solemnly, before God and the World, declare, that, exerting the utmost Energy of those Powers, which our beneficent Creator hath graciously bestowed upon us, the Arms we have been compelled by our Enemies to assume, we will, in defiance of every hazard, with un-abating Firmness and Perseverance, employ for the preservation of our Liberties; being with one Mind resolved to die Freemen rather than to live as Slaves.

Lest this Declaration should disquiet the Minds of our Friends and Fellow-Subjects in any part of the Empire, we assure them that we mean not to dissolve that Union which has so long and so happily subsisted between us, and which we sincerely wish to see restored. Necessity has not yet driven us into that desperate Measure, or induced us to excite any other Nation to War against them. We have not raised Armies with ambitious Designs of separating from Great-Britain, and establishing Independent States. We fight not for Glory or for Conquest. We exhibit to Mankind the remarkable Spectacle of a People attacked by unprovoked Enemies, without any imputation of even suspicion of Offence. They boast of their Privileges and Civilization, and yet proffer no milder Conditions than Servitude of Death.

In our own native Land, in defence of the Freedom that is our Birthright, and which we ever enjoyed till the late Violation of it--for the protection of our Property, acquired solely by the honest Industry of our forefathers and ourselves, against Violence actually offered, we have taken up Arms. We shall lay them down when Hostilities shall cease on the part of the Aggressors, and all danger of their being renewed shall be removed, and not before.

With an humble Confidence in the Mercies of the supreme and impartial Judge and Ruler of the Universe, we most devoutly implore his Divine Goodness to protect us happily through this great Conflict, to dispose our Adversaries to reconciliation on reasonable Terms, and thereby to relieve the Empire from the Calamities of civil War.

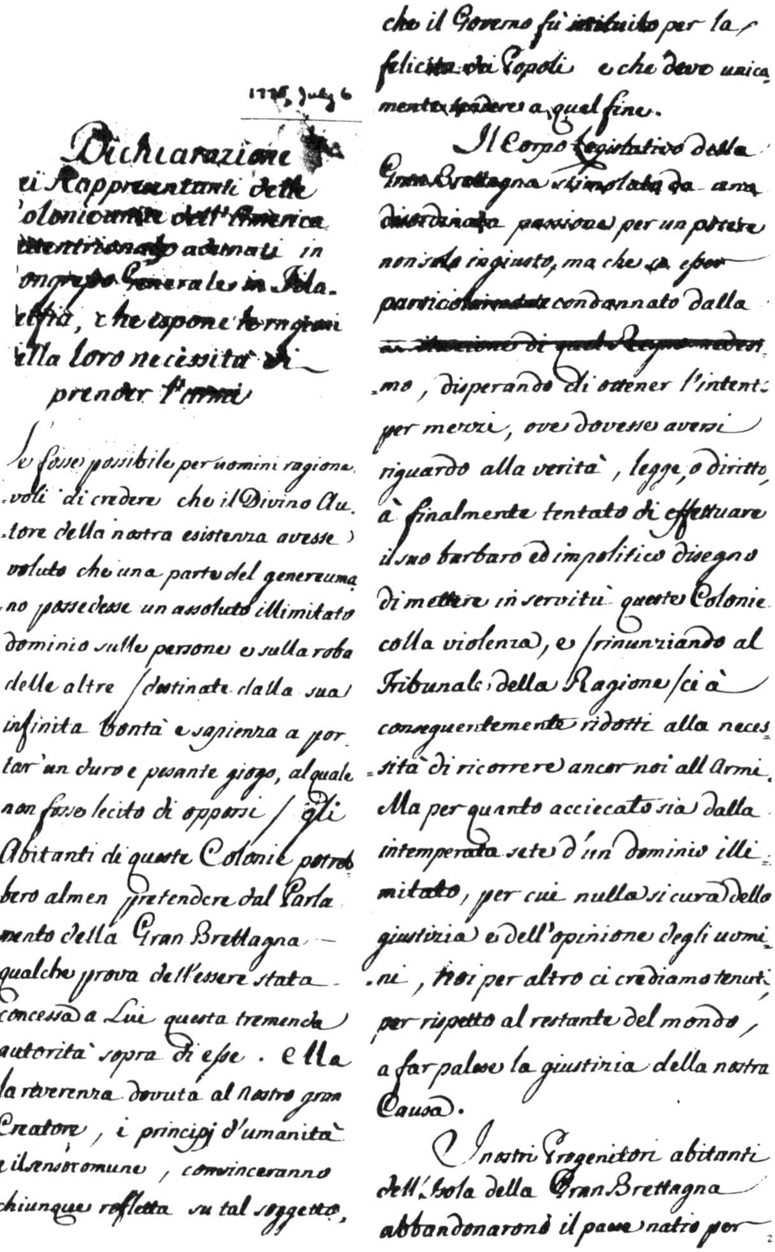

1776, July 6

Dichiarazione dei Rappresentanti delle Colonie unite dell'America settentrionale adunati in Congresso Generale in Filadelfia, che espone i motivi della loro necessità di prender l'armi

Se fosse possibile per uomini ragionevoli di credere che il Divino Autore della nostra esistenza avesse voluto che una parte del genere umano possedesse un assoluto illimitato dominio sulle persone e sulla roba delle altre destinate dalla sua infinita bontà e sapienza a portar un duro e pesante giogo, al quale non fosse lecito di opporsi, gli Abitanti di queste Colonie potrebbero almen pretendere dal Parlamento della Gran Brettagna qualche prova dell'essere stata concessa a Lui questa tremenda autorità sopra di esse. Ma la reverenza dovuta al nostro gran Creatore, i principj d'umanità e il senso comune, convinceranno chiunque rifletta su tal soggetto, che il Governo fu istituito per la felicità dei Popoli e che deve unicamente tendere a quel fine.

Il Corpo Legislativo della Gran Brettagna stimolato da una disordinata passione per un potere non solo ingiusto, ma che sa esser particolarmente condannato dalla costituzione di quel Regno medesimo, disperando di ottener l'intento per mezzi, ove dovesse aversi riguardo alla verità, legge, o diritto, à finalmente tentato di effettuare il suo barbaro ed impolitico disegno di mettere in servitù queste Colonie colla violenza, e rinunziando al Tribunale della Ragione ci à conseguentemente ridotti alla necessità di ricorrere ancor noi all'Armi. Ma per quanto acciecato sia dalla intemperata sete d'un dominio illimitato, per cui nulla si cura della giustizia e dell'opinione degli uomini, noi per altro ci crediamo tenuti per rispetto al restante del mondo, a far palese la giustizia della nostra Causa.

I nostri Progenitori abitanti dell'Isola della Gran Brettagna abbandonarono il paese natio per

(Italian translation by Mazzei, first page)

sotti a quel disperato passo, né ad eccitare altre nazioni contro di Loro. Non abbiamo messo in piede Armate coll'ambiziosa idea di separarci dalla Gran Brettagna, e d'istituire Stati independenti. Non si combatte per gloria o per conquiste. Si espone al Mondo il rimarcabile spettacolo di un Popolo assalito da non provocati nemici, senza la minima imputazione, e nessun sospetto di offesa. Essi vantano i Loro privilegj e la Loro cultura, e poi non offrono condizione più mite che servitù o morte.

Nella nostra propria terra natia, in difesa della libertà nostra per diritto di nascita, e che abbiamo sempre goduta finchè non fu ultimamente violata, per proteggere i nostri Beni unicamente acquistati dall'industria dei nostri Pr[illegible]itori e di noi medesimi, [illegible] violenza ultimamente [illegible]ostrataci, abbiamo prese le [illegible]. Le deporremo quando gli [illegible]sori cesseranno dalle loro [illegible], e che sia rimosso ogni [illegible] ricominciate, e [illegible]prima.

Con umile speranza nella misericordia del supremo imparzia Giudice e Regolatore dell'universo, devotamente imploriamo la sua Divina bontà a volerci felicemente condurre al fine di questa gran contesa, a disporre i nostri Avversarj a riconciliarsi con condizioni ragionevoli, e conseguentemente a sollevar l'Impero dalle calamità d'una guerra civile.

Per ordine del Congresso
Giovanni Hancock Presidente
Carlo Thomson Segretario

[illegible]adelfia 6. Luglio 1775.

(Signature page)

THE DECLARATION OF INDEPENDENCE

In CONGRESS, July 4, 1776.

A DECLARATION

By the REPRESENTATIVES of the

UNITED STATES OF AMERICA

In GENERAL CONGRESS Assembled.

When in the Course of human Events, it becomes necessary for one People to dissolve the Political Bands which have connected them with another, and to assume among the Powers of the Earth, the separate and equal Station to which the Laws of Nature and of Nature's God entitle them, a decent Respect to the Opinions of Mankind requires that they should declare the causes which impel them to the Separation.

We hold these Truths to be self-evident, that all Men are created equal, that they are endowed by their Creator with certain unalienable Rights, that among these are life, Liberty, and the Pursuit of Happiness--That to secure these Rights, Governments are instituted among Men, deriving their just Powers from the Consent of the Governed, that whenever any Form of

Government becomes destructive of these Ends, it is the Right of the People to alter or to abolish it, and to institute new Government, laying its Foundation on such Principles, and organizing its Powers in such Form, as to them shall seem most likely to effect their Safety and Happiness. Prudence, indeed, will dictate that Governments long established should not be changed for light and transient Causes; and accordingly all Experience hath shown, that mankind are more disposed to suffer, while Evils are sufferable, than to right themselves by abolishing the Forms to which they are accustomed. But when a long Train of Abuses and Usurpations, pursuing invariably the same Object, evinces a Design to reduce them under absolute Despotism, it is their Right, it is their Duty, to throw off such Government, and to provide new Guards for their future Security. Such has been the patient Sufferance of these Colonies; and such is now the Necessity which constrains them to alter their former Systems of Government.

The History of the present King of Great-Britain is a History of repeated Injuries and Usurpations, all having in direct Object the Establishment of an absolute Tyranny over these States. To prove this, let Facts be submitted to a candid World:

He has refused his Assent to Laws, the most wholesome and necessary for the public Good.

He has forbidden his Governors to pass Laws of immediate and pressing Importance, unless suspended in their Operation till his Assent should be obtained; and when so suspended, he has utterly neglected to attend to them.

He has refused to pass other Laws for the Accommodation of large Districts of People, unless those People would relinquish the Right of Representation in the Legislature, a Right inestimable to them, and formidable to Tyrants only.

He has called together Legislative Bodies at Places unusual, uncomfortable, and distant from the Depository of their public Records, for the sole Purpose of fatiguing them into Compliance with his Measures.

He has dissolved Representative Houses repeatedly, for opposing with manly Firmness his Invasions on the Rights of the People.

He has refused for a long Time, after such Dissolution, to cause others to be elected; whereby the Legislative Powers, incapable of Annihilation, have returned to the People at large for their exercise; the State remaining in the mean time exposed to all the Dangers of Invasion from without, and Convulsions within.

He has endeavored to prevent the Population of these States; for that purpose obstructing the Laws for Naturalization of Foreigners; refusing to pass others to encourage their Migrations hither, and raising the Conditions of new Appropriations of Lands.

He has obstructed the Administration of Justice, by refusing his Assent to Laws for establishing Judiciary Powers.

He has made Judges dependent on his Will alone, for the Tenure of their Offices, and the Amount and Payment of their Salaries.

He has erected a Multitude of new Offices, and sent hither Swarms of Officers to harass our People, and eat out their Substance.

He has kept among us, in Times of Peace, Standing Armies, without the consent of our Legislatures.

He has affected to render the Military independent of and superior to the Civil Power.

He has combined with others to subject us to a Jurisdiction foreign to our Constitution, and unacknowledged by our Laws; giving his Assent to their Acts of pretended Legislation:

For quartering large Bodies of Armed Troops among us:

For protecting them, by a mock Trial, from Punishment for any Murders which they should commit on the Inhabitants of these States:

For cutting off our Trade with all Parts of the World:

For imposing Taxes on us without our Consent:

For depriving us, in many Cases, of the Benefits of Trial by Jury:

For transporting us beyond Seas to be tried for pretended Offenses:

For abolishing the free System of English Laws in a neighboring Province, establishing therein an arbitrary Government, and enlarging its Boundaries, so as to render it at once an Example and fit Instrument for introducing the same absolute Rule into these Colonies:

For taking away our Charters, abolishing our most valuable Laws, and altering fundamentally the Forms of our Governments:

For suspending our own Legislatures, and declaring themselves invested with Power to legislate for us in all Cases whatsoever.

He has abdicated Government here, by declaring us out of his Protection and waging War against us.

He has plundered our Seas, ravaged our Coasts, burnt our Towns, and destroyed the Lives of our People.

He is, at this Time, transporting large Armies of foreign Mercenaries to complete the Works of Death, Desolation, and Tyranny, already begun with circumstances of Cruelty and Perfidy, scarcely paralleled in the most barbarous Ages, and totally unworthy the Head of a civilized Nation.

He has constrained our fellow Citizens taken Captive on the high Seas to bear Arms against their Country, to become the Executioners of their Friends and Brethren, or to fall themselves by their Hands.

He has excited domestic Insurrections amongst us, and has endeavored to bring on the Inhabitants of our Frontiers, the merciless Indian Savages, whose known rule of Warfare, is an undistinguished Destruction, of all Ages, Sexes and Conditions.

In every stage of these Oppressions we have Petitioned for Redress in the most humble Terms: Our repeated Petitions have been answered only by repeated Injury. A Prince, whose Character is thus marked by every act which may define a Tyrant, is unfit to be the Ruler of a free People.

Nor have we been wanting in Attentions to our British Brethren. We have warned them from Time to Time of Attempts by their Legislature to extend an unwarrantable Jurisdiction over us. We have reminded them of the Circumstances of our Emigration and Settlement here. We have appealed to their native Justice and Magnanimity, and we have conjured them by the Ties of our common Kindred to disavow these Usurpations, which, would inevitably interrupt our Connections and Correspondence. They too have been deaf to the Voice of Justice and of Consanguinity. We must, therefore, acquiesce in the Necessity, which denounces our Separation, and hold them, as we hold the rest of Mankind, Enemies in War, in Peace, Friends.

We, therefore, the Representatives of the UNITED STATES OF AMERICA, in General Congress, Assembled, appealing to the supreme Judge of the World for the Rectitude of our Intentions, do, in the Name, and by Authority of the good People of these Colonies, solemnly Publish and Declare, That these United Colonies are, and of Right ought to be, **Free and Independent States**; that they are absolved from all Allegiance to the British Crown, and that all political Connection between them and the State of Great Britain, is and ought to be totally dissolved; and that as **Free and Independent States**, they have full Power to levy War, conclude Peace, contract Alliances, establish Commerce, and to do all other Acts and Things which **Independent States** may of right do. And for the support of this Declaration, with a firm Reliance on the Protection of divine Providence, we mutually pledge to each other our Lives, our Fortunes, and our sacred Honor.

Signed by ORDER and in BEHALF of the CONGRESS,
JOHN HANCOCK, President.

Attest.
CHARLES THOMSON, Secretary.

Philadelphia: Printed by John Dunlap.

SIGNERS OF THE
DECLARATION OF INDEPENDENCE
According to the Authenticated List Printed by
Order of Congress of January 18, 1777
John Hancock.

New-Hampshire:
Josiah Bartlett, Wm. Whipple
Matthew Thornton

Massachusetts-Bay:
Sam Adams, John Adams
Rob Treat Paine, Elbridge Gerry

Rhodes-Island and Providence, &c:
Step. Hopkins, William Ellery

Connecticut:
Roger Sherman, Sam Huntington
Wm. Williams, Oliver Wolcott

New-York:
Wm. Floyd, Phil. Livingston
Fran. Lewis, Lewis Morris

New-Jersey:
Rich. Stockton, Fno. Witherspoon
Fra. Hopkinson, John Hart, Abra. Clark

Pennsylvania:
Rob. Morris, Benjamin Rush

Benja. Franklin, John Morton
Geo. Clymer, Fa. Smith
Geo. Taylor, James Wilson, Geo. Ross

Delaware:
Caesar Rodney, Geo. Read

Maryland:
Samuel Chase, Wm. Paca
Tho. Stone, Charles Carroll

Virginia:
George Wythe, Richard Henry Lee
Th. Jefferson, Benj. Harrison
Tho. Nelson, jr., Francis Lightfoot Lee
Carter Braxton

North-Carolina:
Wm. Hooper, Joseph Hewes, John Penn

South-Carolina:
Edward Rutledge, Tho. Heyward, jun.
Thomas Lynch, jun., Arthur Middleton

Georgia:
Button Gwinnett, Lyman Hall, Geo. Walton

THE ARTICLES OF CONFEDERATION

THE ARTICLES OF CONFEDERATION

Agreed to by Congress November 15, 1777; ratified and in force, March 1, 1781

TO ALL TO WHOM these Presents shall come, we the undersigned Delegates of the States affixed to our Names send greeting.

Whereas the Delegates of the United States of America in Congress assembled did on the fifteenth day of November in the Year of our Lord One Thousand Seven Hundred and Seventy Seven, and in the Second Year of the Independence of America agree to certain articles of Confederation and perpetual Union between the States of New Hampshire, Massachusetts bay, Rhode Island and Providence Plantations, Connecticut, New York, New Jersey, Pennsylvania, Delaware, Maryland, Virginia, North Carolina, South Carolina and Georgia in the Words following, viz. "Articles of Confederation and perpetual Union between the States of New Hampshire, Massachusetts bay, Rhode Island and Providence Plantations, Connecticut, New York, New Jersey, Pennsylvania, Delaware, Maryland, Virginia, North Carolina, South Carolina and Georgia.

Article I. The Style of this confederacy shall be "The United States of America."

Article II. Each state retains its sovereignty, freedom and independence, and every power, jurisdiction and right, which is not by this Confederation expressly delegated to the United States, in Congress assembled.

Article III. The said States hereby severally enter into a firm league of friendship with each other, for their common defence, the security of their liberties, and their mutual and general welfare, binding themselves to assist each other, against all force offered to, or attacks made upon them, or any of them, on account of religion, sovereignty, trade, or any other pretence whatever.

Article IV. The better to secure and perpetuate mutual friendship and intercourse among the people of the different States in this Union, the free inhabitants of each of these States, paupers, vagabonds and fugitives from justice excepted, shall be entitled to all privileges and immunities of free citizens in the several States; and the people of each state shall have free ingress and regress to and from any other State, and shall enjoy therein all the privileges of trade and commerce, subject to the same duties, impositions and restrictions as the inhabitants thereof respectively, provided that such restriction shall not extend so far as to prevent the removal of property imported into any state, to any other state of which the Owner is an inhabitant; provided also that no imposition, duties or restriction shall be laid by any state, on the property of the United States, or either of them.

If any person guilty of or charged with treason, felony, or other high misdemeanor in any state, shall flee from Justice, and be found in any of the United States, he shall upon demand of the governor or executive power of the state from which he fled, be delivered up and removed to the State having jurisdiction of his offence.

Full faith and credit shall be given in each of these States to the records, acts and judicial proceedings of the courts and magistrates of every other state.

Article V. For the more convenient management of the general interests of the United States, delegates shall be annually appointed in such manner as the legislature of each state shall direct, to meet in Congress on the first Monday in November, in every year, with a power reserved to each state, to recall its delegates, or any of them, at any time within the year, and to send others in their stead, for the remainder of the year.

No state shall be represented in Congress by less than two, nor by more than seven Members; and no person shall be capable of being a delegate for more than three years in any term of six years; nor shall any person, being a delegate, be capable of holding any office under the United States, for which he, or another for his benefit receives any salary, fees or emolument of any kind.

Each state shall maintain its own delegates in a meeting of the States, and while they act as members of the committee of the States.

In determining questions in the United States, in Congress assembled, each State shall have one vote.

Freedom of speech and debate in Congress shall not be impeached or questioned in any Court, or place out of Congress, and the members of Congress shall be protected in their persons from arrests and imprisonments, during the time of their going to and from, and attendance on Congress, except for treason, felony, or breach of the peace.

Article VI. No state without the Consent of the United States in Congress assembled, shall send any embassy to, or receive any embassy from, or enter into any conference, agreement, or alliance or treaty with any king, prince or state; nor shall any person holding any office of profit or trust under the United States, or any of them, accept of any present, emolument, office or title of any kind whatever from any king, prince or foreign state; nor shall the United States in Congress assembled, or any of them, grant any title of nobility.

No two or more States shall enter into any treaty, confederation or alliance whatever between them, without the consent of the United States in Congress assembled, specifying accurately the purposes for which the same is to be entered into, and how long it shall continue.

No state shall lay any imposts or duties, which may interfere with any stipulations in treaties, entered into by the United States in Congress assembled, with any king, prince or state, in pursuance of any treaties already proposed by Congress, to the courts of France and Spain.

No vessels of war shall be kept up in time of peace by any State, except such number only, as shall be deemed necessary by the United States in Congress assembled, for the defence of such State or its trade;

nor shall any body of forces be kept up by any State, in time of peace, except such number only, as in the judgment of the United States in Congress assembled, shall be deemed requisite to garrison the forts necessary for the defence of such State; but every State shall always keep up a well regulated and disciplined militia, sufficiently armed and accoutered, and shall provide and constantly have ready for use, in public stores, a due number of field pieces and tents, and a proper quantity of arms, ammunition and camp equipage.

No state shall engage in any war without the consent of the United States in Congress assembled, unless such state be actually invaded by enemies, or shall have received certain advice of a resolution being formed by some nation of Indians to invade such State, and the danger is so imminent as not to admit of a delay, till the United States in Congress assembled can be consulted: nor shall any state grant commissions to any ships or vessels of war, nor letters of marque or reprisal, except it be after a declaration of war by the United States in Congress assembled, and then only against the kingdom or State and the subjects thereof, against which war has been so declared, and under such regulations as shall be established by the United States in Congress assembled, unless such state be infested by pirates, in which case vessels of war may be fitted out for that occasion, and kept so long as the danger shall continue, or until the United States in Congress assembled shall determine otherwise.

Article VII. When land forces are raised by any state for the common defence, all officers of or under the rank of colonel, shall be appointed by the legislature of each state respectively by whom such forces shall be raised, or in such manner as such state shall direct, and all vacancies shall be filled up by the state which first made the appointment.

Article VIII. All charges of war, and all other expenses that shall be incurred for the common defence or general welfare, and allowed by the United States in Congress assembled, shall be defrayed out of a common treasury, which shall be supplied by the several States, in proportion to the value of all land within each state, granted to or surveyed for any person, as such land and the buildings and improvements thereon shall be estimated according to such mode as the United States in Congress assembled, shall from time to time direct and appoint. The taxes for paying that proportion shall be laid and levied by the authority and direction of the legislatures of the several States within the time agreed upon by the United States in Congress assembled.

Article IX. The United States in Congress assembled, shall have the sole and exclusive right and power of determining on peace and war, except in the cases mentioned in the sixth article--of sending and receiving ambassadors--entering into treaties and alliances, provided that no treaty of commerce shall be made whereby the legislative power of the respective States shall be restrained from imposing such imposts and duties on foreigners, as their own people are subjected to, or from prohibiting the exportation or importation of any species of goods or commodities whatsoever--of establishing rules for deciding in all cases, what captures on land or water shall be legal, and in what manner prizes taken by land or naval forces in the service of the United States shall be divided or appropriated--of granting letters of marque and reprisal in times of peace--appointing courts for the trial of piracies and felonies committed on the high seas and establishing courts for receiving and determining finally appeals in all cases of captures, provided that no member of Congress shall be appointed a judge of any of the said courts.

The United States in Congress assembled shall also be the last resort on appeal in all disputes and differences now subsisting or that hereafter may arise between two or more States concerning boundary, jurisdiction or any other cause whatever; which authority shall always be exercised in the manner following:

Whenever the legislative or executive authority or lawful agent State in controversy with another shall present a petition to Congress, stating the matter in question and praying for a hearing, notice thereof shall be given by order of Congress to the legislative or executive authority of the other State in controversy, and a day assigned for the appearance of the parties by their lawful agents, who shall then be directed to appoint by joint consent, commissioners or judges to constitute a court for hearing and determining the matter in question; but if they cannot agree, Congress shall name three persons out of each of the United States, and from the list of such persons each party shall alternately strike out one, the petitioners beginning, until the number shall be reduced to thirteen; and from that number not less than seven, nor more than nine names as Congress shall direct, shall in the presence of Congress be drawn out by lot, and the persons whose names shall be so drawn or any five of them, shall be commissioners or judges, to hear and finally determine the controversy, so always as a major part of the judges who shall hear the cause shall agree in the determination: and if either party shall neglect to attend at the day appointed, without showing reasons, which Congress shall judge sufficient, or being present shall refuse to strike, the Congress shall proceed to nominate three persons out of each State, and the Secretary of Congress shall strike in behalf of such party absent or refusing; and the judgment and sentence of the court to be appointed, in the manner before prescribed, shall be final and conclusive; and if any of the parties shall refuse to submit to the authority of such court, or to appear to defend their claim or cause, the court shall nevertheless proceed to pronounce sentence, or judgment, which shall in like manner be final and decisive, the judgment or sentence and other proceedings being in either case transmitted to Congress, and lodged among the acts of Congress for the security of the parties concerned: provided that every commissioner, before he sits in judgment, shall take an oath to be administered by one of the judges of the supreme or superior court of the state, where the cause shall be tried, "well and truly to hear and determine the matter in question, according to the best of his judgment, without favor, affection or hope of reward;" provided also that no State shall be deprived of territory for the benefit of the United States.

All controversies concerning the private right of soil claimed under different grants of two or more States, whose jurisdictions as they may respect such lands, and the States which passed such grants are adjusted, the said grants or either of them being at the same time claimed to have originated antecedent to such settlement of jurisdiction, shall on the petition of either party to the Congress of the United States, be finally determined as near as may be in the same manner as is before prescribed for deciding disputes respecting territorial jurisdiction between different States.

The United States in Congress assembled shall also have the sole and exclusive right and power of regulating the alloy and value of coin struck by their own authority, or by that of the respective States, fixing the standard of weights and measures throughout the United States, regulating the trade and managing all affairs with the Indians, not members of any of the States, provided that the legislative right of any state within its own limits be not infringed or violated, or establishing and regulating post offices from one State to another, throughout all the United States, and exacting such postage on the papers passing through the same as may be requisite to defray the expenses of the said office appointing all officers of the land forces, in the service of the United States, excepting regimental officers, or appointing all the officers of the naval forces, and commissioning all officers whatever in the service of the United States, or making rules for the government and regulation of the said land and naval forces, and directing their operations.

The United States in Congress assembled shall have authority to appoint a committee, to sit in the recess of Congress, to be denominated "A Committee of the States," and to consist of one delegate from each state; and to appoint such other committees and civil officers as may be necessary for managing the general affairs of the United States under their direction, to appoint one of their number to preside, provided that no person be allowed to serve in the office of president more than one year in any term of three years; to ascertain the necessary sums of Money to be raised for the service of the United States, and to appropriate and apply the same for defraying the public expenses, or to borrow money, or emit bills on the credit of the United States, transmitting every half year to the respective States an account of the sums of money so borrowed or emitted, to build and equip a navy, to agree upon the number of land forces, and to make requisitions from each state for its quota, in proportion to the number of white inhabitants in such state; which requisition shall be binding, and thereupon the legislature of each State shall appoint the regimental officers, raise the men and clothe, arm and equip them in a soldier like manner, at the expense of the United States, and the officers and men so clothed, armed and equipped shall march to the place appointed, and within the time agreed on by the United States in Congress assembled. But if the United States in Congress assembled shall, on consideration of circumstances judge proper that any State should not raise men, or should raise a smaller number than its quota, and that any other state should raise a greater number of men than the quota thereof, such extra number shall be raised, officered, clothed, armed and equipped in the same manner as the quota of such State, unless the legislature of such state shall judge that such extra number cannot be safely spared out of the same, in which case they shall raise officer, clothe, arm and equip as many of such extra number as they judge can be safely spared. And the officers and men so clothed, armed and equipped, shall march to the place appointed, and within the time agreed on by the United States in Congress assembled.

The United States in Congress assembled shall never engage in a war, nor grant letters of marque and reprisal in time of peace, nor enter into any treaties or alliances, nor coin money, nor regulate the value thereof, nor ascertain the sums and expenses necessary for the defence and welfare of the United States, or any of them, nor emit bills, nor borrow money on the credit of the United States, nor appropriate money, nor agree upon the number of vessels of war, to be built or purchased, or the number of land or sea forces to be raised, nor appoint a commander-in-chief of the army or navy, unless nine States assent to the same: nor shall a question on any other point, except for adjourning from day to day be determined, unless by the votes of a majority of the United States in Congress assembled.

The Congress of the United States shall have power to adjourn to any time within the year, and to any place within the United States, so that no period of adjournment be for a longer duration than the space of six months, and shall publish the journal of their proceedings monthly, except such parts thereof relating to treaties, alliances or military operations as in their judgment require secrecy; and the yeas and nays of the delegates of each state on any question shall be entered on the journal, when it is desired by any delegate; and the delegates of a State, or any of them, at his or their request shall be furnished with a transcript of the said journal, except such parts as are above excepted, to lay before the legislatures of the several States.

Article X. The Committee of the States, or any nine of them, shall be authorized to execute, in the recess of Congress, such of the powers of Congress as the

United States in Congress assembled, by the consent of nine States, shall from time to time think expedient to vest them with; provided that no power be delegated to the said Committee, for the exercise of which, by the Articles of Confederation, the voice of nine States in the Congress of the United States assembled is requisite.

Article XI. Canada acceding to this Confederation, and joining in the measures of the United States, shall be admitted into, and entitled to all the advantages of this Union: but no other colony shall be admitted into the same, unless such admission be agreed to by nine States.

Article XII. All bills of credit emitted, monies borrowed and debts contracted by, or under the authority of Congress, before the assembling of the United States, in pursuance of the present Confederation, shall be deemed and considered as a charge against the United States, for payment and satisfaction whereof the said United States, and the public faith are hereby solemnly pledged.

Article XIII. Every State shall abide by the determinations of the United States in Congress assembled, on all questions which by this Confederation are submitted to them. And the Articles of this Confederation shall be inviolably observed by every state, and the union shall be perpetual; nor shall any alteration at any time hereafter be made in any of them; unless such alteration be agreed to in a Congress of the United States, and be afterwards confirmed by the legislatures of every State.

AND WHEREAS it hath pleased the Great Governor of the World to incline the hearts of the legislatures we respectively represent in Congress, to approve of, and to authorize us to ratify the said Articles of Confederation and perpetual Union, KNOW YE that we the undersigned delegates, by virtue of the power and authority to us given for that purpose, do by these presents, in the name and in behalf of our respective constituents, fully and entirely ratify and confirm each and every of the said Articles of Confederation and perpetual Union, and all and singular the matters and things therein contained: And we do further solemnly plight and engage the faith of our respective constituents, that they shall abide by the determinations of the United States in Congress assembled, on all questions, which by the said Confederation are submitted to them. And that the Articles thereof shall be inviolably observed by the States we respectively represent, and that the Union shall be perpetual. In Witness whereof we have hereunto set our hands in Congress. Done at Philadelphia in the state of Pennsylvania the ninth Day of July in the Year of our Lord One Thousand Seven Hundred and Seventy-eight, and in the third year of the Independence of America.

On the part and behalf of the State of New Hampshire:

JOSIAH BARTLETT
JOHN WENTWORTH JUNR.
August 8th 1778

On the part and behalf of The State of Massachusetts Bay:

JOHN HANCOCK
SAMUEL ADAMS
FRANCIS DANA
JAMES LOVELL

ELBRIDGE GERRY
SAMUEL HOLTEN

On the part and behalf of the State of Rhode Island and Providence Plantations:

WILLIAM ELLERY
JOHN COLLINS
HENRY MARCHANT

On the part and behalf of the State of Connecticut:

ROGER SHERMAN
TITUS HOSMER
SAMUEL HUNTINGTON
ANDREW ADAMS
OLIVER WOLCOTT

On the Part and Behalf of the State of New York:

JAMES DUANE
WM DUER
FRANCIS LEWIS
GOUV MORRIS

On the Part and in Behalf of the State of New Jersey, November 26, 1778.

JNO WITHERSPOON
NATHANIEL SCUDDER

On the part and behalf of the State of Pennsylvania:

ROBT MORRIS
WILLIAM CLINGAN
DANIEL ROBERDEAU
JOSEPH REED
JOHN BAYARD SMITH
22nd July 1778

On the part and behalf of the State of Delaware:

THO McKEAN
February 12, 1779
JOHN DICKINSON
May 5th 1779
NICHOLAS VAN DYKE

On the part and behalf of the State of Maryland:
JOHN HANSON
March 1 1781
DANIEL CARROLL DO

On the Part and Behalf of the State of Virginia:
RICHARD HENRY LEE JNO HARVIE
JOHN BANISTER FRANCIS LIGHTFOOT LEE
THOMAS ADAMS

On the part and Behalf of the State of No Carolina:
JOHN PEN
July 21st 1778
CORNS HARNETT
JNO WILLIAMS

On the part and behalf of the State of South Carolina:
HENRY LAURENS RICHD HUTSON
WILLIAM H DRAYTON THOS HEYWARD JUNR
JNO MATHEWS

On the part and behalf of the State of Georgia:
JNO WALTON
24th July 1778
EDWD TELFAIR
EDWD LANGWORTHY

THE CONSTITUTION OF THE UNITED STATES OF AMERICA

We, the People of the United States, in order to form a more perfect union, establish justice, insure domestic tranquility, provide for the common defence, promote the general welfare, and secure the blessings of liberty to ourselves and our posterity, do ordain and establish this Constitution for the United States of America.

ARTICLE I.

Sect. 1. ALL legislative powers herein granted shall be vested in a Congress of the United States, which shall consist of a Senate and House of Representatives.

Sect 2. The House of Representatives shall be composed of members chosen every second year by the people of the several states, and the electors in each state shall have the qualifications requisite for electors of the most numerous branch of the state legislature.

No person shall be a representative who shall not have attained to the age of twenty-five years, and been seven years a citizen of the United States, and who shall not, when elected, be an inhabitant of that state in which he shall be chosen.

[Representatives and direct taxes shall be apportioned among the several states which may be included within this Union, according to their respective numbers, which shall be determined by adding to the whole number of free persons, including those bound to service for a term of years, and excluding Indians not taxed, three-fifths of all other persons.] (The part enclosed in brackets was changed by section 2 of Amendment XIV.) The actual enumeration shall be made within three years after the first meeting of Congress of the United States, and within every subsequent term of ten years, in such manner as they shall by law direct. The number of representatives shall not exceed one for every thirty thousand, but each state shall have at least one representative; and until such enumeration shall be made, the state of New-Hampshire shall be entitled to choose three, Massachusetts eight, Rhode-Island and Providence Plantation one, Connecticut five, New-York six, New Jersey four, Pennsylvania eight, Delaware one, Maryland six, Virginia ten, North-Carolina five, South-Carolina five, and Georgia three.

When vacancies happen in the representation from any state, the Executive authority thereof shall issue writs of election to fill such vacancies.

The House of Representatives shall choose their Speaker and other officers; and shall have the sole power of impeachment.

Sect 3. The Senate of the United States shall be composed of two senators from each state, [chosen by the legislature thereof,] *(The clause enclosed by brackets was changed by clause 1 of Amendment XVII.)* for six years; and each senator shall have one vote.

Immediately after they shall be assembled in consequence of the first election, they shall be divided as equally as may be into three classes. The seats of the senators of the first class shall be vacated at the expiration of the second year, of the second class at the expiration of the fourth year, and of the third class at the expiration of the sixth year, so that one-third may be chosen every second year; [and if vacancies happen by resignation, or otherwise, during the recess of the Legislature of any state, the Executive thereof may make temporary appointments until the next meeting of the Legislature, which shall then fill such vacancies.]

(The part enclosed by brackets was changed by clause 2 of Amendment XVII.)

No person shall be a senator who shall not have attained to the age of thirty years, and been nine years a citizen of the United States, and who shall not, when elected, be an inhabitant of that state for which he shall be chosen.

The Vice-President of the United States shall be President of the senate, but shall have no vote, unless they be equally divided.

The Senate shall choose their officers, and also a President pro tempore, in the absence of the Vice-President, or when he shall exercise the office of President of the United States.

The Senate shall have the sole power to try all impeachments. When sitting for that purpose, they shall be on oath or affirmation. When the President of the United States is tried, the Chief Justice shall preside: And no person shall be convicted without the concurrence of two-thirds of the members present.

Judgment in cases of impeachment shall not extend further than to removal from office, and disqualification to hold and enjoy any office of honor, trust or profit under the United States; but the party convicted shall nevertheless be liable and subject to indictment, trial, judgment and punishment, according to law.

Sect. 4 The times, places and manner of holding elections for senators and representatives, shall be prescribed in each state by the legislature thereof; but the Congress may at any time by law make or alter such regulations, except as to places of choosing Senators.

The Congress shall assemble at least once in every year, and such meeting shall [be on the first Monday in

December,] *(The clause enclosed by brackets was changed by section 2 of Amendment XX.)* unless they shall by law appoint a different day.

Sect 5. Each House shall be the judge of the elections, returns and qualifications of its own members, and a majority of each shall constitute a quorum to do business; but a smaller number may adjourn from day to day, and may be authorized to compel the attendance of absent members, in such manner, and under such penalties as each house may provide.

Each house may determine the rules of its proceedings, punish its members for disorderly behavior, and, with the concurrence of two-thirds, expel a member.

Each house shall keep a journal of its proceedings, and from time to time publish the same, excepting such parts as may in their judgment require secrecy; and the yeas and nays of the members o either house on any question shall, at the desire of one-fifth of those present, be entered on the journal.

Neither house, during the session of Congress, shall, without the consent of the other, adjourn for more than three days, nor to any other place than that in which the two houses shall be sitting.

Sect. 6. The senators and representatives shall receive a compensation for their services, to be ascertained by law, and paid out of the treasury of the United States. They shall in all cases, except treason, felony and breach of the peace, be privileged from arrest during their attendance at the session of their respective houses, and in going to and returning from the same; and for any speech or debate in either house, they shall not be questioned in any other place.

No senator or representative shall, during the time for which he was elected, be appointed to any civil office under the authority of the United States, which shall have been created, or the emoluments whereof shall have been increased during such time; and no person holding any office under the United States, shall be a member of either house during his continuance in office.

Sect. 7. All bills for raising revenues shall originate in the house of representatives; but the senate may propose or concur with amendments as on other bills.

Every bill which shall have passed the house of representatives and the senate, shall, before it become a law, be presented to the president of the United States; if he approve he shall sign it, but if not he shall return it, with his objections to that house in which i shall have originated, who shall enter the objections at large on their journal, and proceed to reconsider it. If after such reconsideration two-thirds of that house shall agree to pass the bill, it shall be sent, together with the objections, to the other house, by which it shall likewise be reconsidered, and if approved by two-thirds of that house, it shall become a law. But in all such cases the votes of both house shall be determined by yeas and nays, and the names of the persons voting for and against the bill shall be entered on the journal of each house respectively. If any bill shall not be returned by the President within ten days (Sunday excepted) after it shall have been presented to him, the same shall be a law, in like manner as if he had signed it, unless the Congress by their adjournment prevent its return, in which case it shall not be a law.

Every order, resolution, or vote to which the concurrent of the Senate and House of Representatives may be necessary (except on a question of adjournment) shall be presented to the President of the United States;

and before the same shall take effect, shall be approved by him, or, being disapproved by him, shall be repassed by two-thirds of the Senate and House of Representatives, according to the rules and limitations prescribed in the case of a bill.

Sect. 8. The Congress shall have power

To lay and collect taxes, duties, imposts and excises, to pay the debts and provide for the common defence and general welfare of the United States; but all duties, imposts and excises shall be uniform throughout the United States.

To borrow money on the credit of the United States;

To regulate commerce with foreign nations, and among the several states, and with the Indian tribes;

To establish an uniform rule of naturalization, and uniform laws on the subject of bankruptcies throughout the United States;

To coin money, regulate the value thereof, and of foreign coin, and fix the standard weights and measures;

To provide for the punishment of counterfeiting the securities and current coin of the United States;

To establish post offices and post roads;

To promote the progress of science and useful arts, by securing for limited times to authors and inventors the exclusive right to their respective writings and discoveries;

To constitute tribunals inferior to the supreme court;

To define and punish piracies and felonies committed on the high seas, and offenses against the law of nations;

To declare war, grant letters of marque and reprisal, and make rules concerning captures on land and water;

To raise and support armies, but no appropriation of money to that use shall be for a longer term than two years;

To provide and maintain a navy;

To make rules for the government and regulation of the land and naval forces;

To provide for calling forth the militia to execute the laws of the union, suppress insurrections and repel invasions;

To provide for organizing, arming, and disciplining, the militia, and for governing such part of them as may be employed in the service of the United States, reserving to the States respectively, the appointment of the officers, and the authority of training the militia according to the discipline prescribed by Congress.

To exercise exclusive legislation in all cases whatsoever, over such district (not exceeding ten miles square) as may, by cession of particular States, and the acceptance of Congress, become the seat of the government of the United States, and to exercise like authority over all places purchased by the consent of the legislature of the state in which the same shall be, for the erection of forts, magazines, arsenals, dock-yards, and other needful buildings;--And

To make all laws which shall be necessary and proper for carrying into execution the foregoing powers, and all other powers vested by this constitution in the government of the United States, or in any department or officer thereof.

Sect. 9. The migration or importation of such persons as any of the states now existing shall think proper to admit, shall not be prohibited by the Congress prior to the year one thousand eight hundred and eight, but a tax or duty may be imposed on such importation, not exceeding ten dollars for each person.

The privilege of the writ of habeas corpus shall not be suspended unless when in cases of rebellion or invasion the public safety may require it.

No bill of attainder or ex post facto law shall be passed.

No capitation, or other direct, tax shall be laid, unless in proportion to the census or enumeration herein before directed to be taken. *(See also Amendment XVI.)*

No tax or duty shall b laid on articles exported from any state. No preference shall be given by any regulation of commerce or revenue to the ports of one state over those of another: nor shall vessels bound to, or from, one state, be obliged to enter, clear, or pay duties in another.

No money shall be drawn from the treasury, but in consequence of appropriations made by law; and a regular statement and account of the receipts and expenditures of all public money shall be published from time to time.

No title of nobility shall be granted by the United States:--And no person holding any office of profit or trust under them, shall, without consent of the Congress, accept of any present, emolument, office, or title, of any king whatever, from any king, prince, or foreign state.

Sect. 10. No state shall enter into any treaty, alliance, or confederation; grant letters of marque and reprisal; coin money; emit bills of credit; make any thing but gold and silver coin a tender in payment of debts; pass any bill of attainder, ex post facto law, or law impairing the obligation of contracts, or grant any title of nobility.

No state shall, without the consent of the Congress, lay any imposts or duties on imports or exports, except what may be absolutely necessary for executing its inspection laws; and the net produce of all duties and imposts, laid by any state on imports or exports, shall be for the use of the Treasury of the United States; and all such laws shall be subject to the revision and control of the Congress. No state shall, without the consent of Congress, lay any duty of tonnage, keep troops, or ships of war in time of peace, enter into any agreement or compact with another state, or with a foreign power, or engage in war, unless actually invaded, or in such imminent danger as will not admit of delay.

II.

Sect. i. The executive power shall be vested in a president of the United States of America. He shall hold his office during the term of four years, and, together with the vice-resident, chosen for the same term, be elected as follows.

Each state shall appoint, in such manner as the legislature thereof may direct, a number of electors, equal to the whole number of senators and representatives to which the state may be entitled in the Congress: but no senator or representative, or person holding an office of trust or profit under the United States, shall be appointed an elector.

[The electors shall meet in their respective states, and vote by ballot for two persons, of whom one at least shall not be an inhabitant of the same state with themselves. And they shall make a list of all the persons voted for, and of the number of votes for each; which list they shall sign and certify, and transmit sealed to the seat of the government of the United States, directed to the president of the senate. The president of the senate shall, in the presence of the senate and house of representatives, open all the certificates, and the votes shall then be counted. The person having the greatest number of votes shall be the president, if such number be a majority of the whole number of electors appointed; and if there be more than one who have such majority, and have an equal number of votes, then the house of representatives shall immediately choose by ballot one of them for president; and if no person have a majority, then from the five highest on the list the said house shall in like manner choose the president. But in choosing the president, the votes shall be taken by states, the representation from each state having one vote; a quorum for this purpose shall consist of a member or members from two-thirds of the states, and a majority of all the states shall be necessary to a choice. In every case, after the choice of the president, the person having the greatest number of votes of the electors shall be the vice-president. But if there should remain two or more who have equal votes, the senate shall choose from them by ballot the vice-president.] *(This paragraph has been superseded by Amendment XII.)*

The Congress may determine the time of chusing the electors, and the day on which they shall give their votes; which day shall be the same throughout the United States.

No person except a natural born citizen, or a citizen of the United States, at the time of the adoption of this constitution, shall be eligible to the office of president;

neither shall any person be eligible to that office who shall not have attained to the age of thirty-five years, and been fourteen years a resident within the United States.

In case of the removal of the president from office, or of his death, resignation, or inability to discharge the powers and duties of the said office, the same shall devolve on the vice-president, and the Congress may by law provide for the case of removal, death, resignation or inability, both of the president and vice-president, declaring what officer shall then act as president, and such office shall act accordingly, until the disability be removed, or a president shall be elected. *(This clause has been affected by Amendment XXV.)*

The president shall, at stated times, receive for his services, a compensation, which shall neither be increased nor diminished during the period for which he shall have been elected, and he shall not receive within that period any other emolument from the United States, or any of them.

Before he enter on the execution of his office, he shall take the following oath or affirmation:

"I do solemnly swear (or affirm) that I will faithfully execute the office of president of the United States, and will to the best of my ability, preserve, protect and defend the constitution of the United States."

Sect. 2. The president shall be commander in chief of the army and navy of the United States, and of the militia of the several States, when called into the actual service of the United States; he may require the opinion, in writing, of the principal officer in each of the executive departments, upon any subject relating to the duties of their respective offices, and he shall have power to grant reprieves and pardons for offenses against the United States, except in cases of impeachment.

He shall have power, by and with the advice and consent of the senate, to make treaties, provided two-thirds of the senators present concur; and he shall nominate, and by and with the advice and consent of the senate, shall appoint ambassadors, other public ministers and counsels, judges of the supreme court, and all other officers of the United States, whose appointments are not herein otherwise provided for, and which shall be established by law. But the Congress may by law vest the appointment of such inferior officers, as they think proper, in the president alone, in the courts of law, or in the heads of departments.

The president shall have power to fill up all vacancies that may happen during recess of the senate, by granting commissions which shall expire at the end of their next session.

Sect. 3. he shall from time to time give to the Congress information of the state of the union, and recommended to their consideration such measures as he shall judge necessary and expedient; he may, on extraordinary occasions, convene both houses, or either of them, and in case of disagreement between them, with respect to the time of adjournment, he may adjourn them to such time as he shall think proper; he shall receive ambassadors and other public ministers; he shall take care that the laws be faithfully executed, and shall commission all the officers of the United States.

Sect. 4. The president, vice-president and all civil officers of the United States, shall be removed from office on impeachment for, and conviction of, treason, bribery, or other high crimes and misdemeanors.

III.

Sect. 1. The judicial power of the United States, shall be vested in one supreme court, and in such inferior courts as the Congress may from time to time ordain and establish. The judges, both of the supreme and inferior courts, shall hold their offices during good behavior, and shall, at stated times, receive for their services, a compensation, which shall not be diminished during their continuance in office.

Sect 2. The judicial power shall extend to all cases, in law and equity, arising under this constitution, the laws of the United States, and treaties made, or which shall be made, under their authority; to all cases affecting ambassadors, other public ministers and consuls; to all cases of admiralty and maritime jurisdiction; to controversies to which the United States shall be a party; to controversies between two or more States, between a state and citizens of another state, *(This clause has been affected by Amendment XI.)* between citizens of different States, between citizens of the same state claiming lands under grants of different States, and between a state, or the citizens thereof, and foreign States, citizens or subjects.

In all cases affecting ambassadors, other public ministers and consuls, and those in which a state shall be party, the supreme court shall have original jurisdiction. In all the other cases before mentioned, the supreme court shall have appellate jurisdiction, both as to law and fact, with such exceptions, and under such regulations as the Congress shall make.

The trial of all crimes, except in cases of impeachment, shall be by jury; and such trial shall be held in the state where the said crimes shall have been committed; but when not committed within any state, the trial shall be at such place or places as the Congress may by law have directed.

Sect. 3. Treason against the United States, shall consist only in levying war against them, or in adhering to their enemies, giving them aid and comfort. No person shall be convicted of treason unless on the testimony of two witnesses to the same overt act, or on confession in open court.

The congress shall have power to declare the punishment of treason, but no attainder of treason shall work corruption of blood, or forfeiture except during the life of the person attainted.

IV.

Sect. 1. Full faith and credit shall be given in each state to the public acts, records, and judicial proceedings of every other state. And the Congress may by general laws prescribe the manner in which such acts, records and proceedings shall be proved, and the effect thereof.

Sect. 2. The citizens of each state shall be entitled to all privileges and immunities of citizens in the several states.

A person charged in any state with treason, felony, or other crime, who shall flee from justice, and be found in another state, shall, on demand of the executive authority of the state from which he fled, be delivered up, to be removed to the state having jurisdiction of the crime.

[No person held to service or labor in one state, under the laws thereof, escaping into another, shall, in consequence of any laws or regulation therein, be discharged from such service or labor, but shall be delivered up on claim of the party to whom such service or labor may be due.] *(This paragraph has been superseded by Amendment XIII.)*

Sect. 3. New states may be admitted by the Congress into this union; but no new state shall be formed or erected within the jurisdiction of any other state; nor any state be formed by the junction of two or more states, or part of states, without the consent of the legislatures of the states concerned as well as of the Congress.

The Congress shall have power to dispose of and make all needful rules and regulations respecting the territory or other property belonging to the United States; and nothing in this Constitution shall be so construed as to prejudice any claims of the United States, or of any particular state.

Sect. 4. The United States shall guarantee to every state in this union a Republican form of government, and shall protect each of them against invasion; and on application of the legislature, or of the executive (when the legislature cannot be convened) against domestic violence.

V.

The Congress, whenever two-thirds of both houses shall deem it necessary, shall propose amendments to this constitution, or, on the application of the legislatures of two-thirds of the several states, shall call a convention for proposing amendments, which, in either case, shall be valid to all intents and purposes, as part of this constitution, when ratified by the legislatures of three-fourths of the several states, or by conventions in three-fourths thereof, as the one or the other mode of ratification may be proposed by the Congress; Provided, that no amendment which may be made prior to the year one thousand eight hundred and eight shall in any manner affect the first and fourth clauses in the ninth section of the first article; and that no state, without its consent, shall be deprived of its equal suffrage in the senate.

VI.

All debts contracted and engagements entered into, before the adoption of this Constitution, shall be as valid against the United States under this Constitution, as under the confederation.

The constitution, and the laws of the United States which shall be made in pursuance thereof; and all treaties made, or which shall be made, under the authority of the United States, shall be the supreme law of the land; and the judges in every state shall be bound thereby, any thing in the constitution or laws of any state to the contrary notwithstanding.

The senators and representatives before mentioned, and the members of the several state legislatures, and all executive and judicial officers, both of the United States and of the several States, shall be bound by oath or affirmation, to support this constitution; but no religious test shall ever be required as a qualification to any office or public trust under the United States.

VII.

The ratification of the conventions of nine States, shall be sufficient for the establishment of this constitution between the States so ratifying the same.

Done in Convention, by the unanimous consent of the States present, the seventeenth day of September, in the year of our Lord one thousand seven hundred and eighty-seven, and of the Independence of the United States of America the twelfth. In witness whereof we have hereunto subscribed our Names.

GEORGE WASHINGTON, President,
And Deputy from Virginia.

New-Hampshire: *John Langdon, Nicholas Gilman.*
Massachusetts: *Nathaniel Gorham, Rufus King.*
Connecticut: *William S. Johnson, Roger Sherman.*
New-York: *Alexander Hamilton.*
New-Jersey: *William Livingston, David Brearley, William Paterson, Jonathan Dayton.*
Pennsylvania: *Benjamin Franklin, Thomas Mifflin, Robert Morris, George Clymer, Thomas Fitzsimons, Jared Ingersoll, James Wilson, Gouverneur Morris.*
Delaware: *George Read, Gunning Bedford, Jr., John Dickinson, Richard Bassett, Jacob Brown.*
Maryland: *James M'Henry, Daniel of St. Tho., Daniel Carrol.*
Virginia: *John Blair, James Madison, Jr.*
North-Carolina: *William Blount, Richard Dobbs Spaight, Hugh Williamson.*
South-Carolina: *John Rutledge, Charles C. Pinckney, Charles Pinckney, Pierce Butler.*
Georgia: *William Few, Abraham Baldwin.*
Attest, *William Jackson,* Secretary.

In CONVENTION, Monday September 17th, 1787.

PRESENT

The States of New Hampshire, Massachusetts, Connecticut, Mr. Hamilton from New York, New Jersey, Pennsylvania, Delaware, Maryland, Virginia, North Carolina, South Carolina and Georgia:

RESOLVED,

That the preceding Constitution be laid before the United States in Congress assembled, and that it is the opinion of this Convention, that it should afterwards be submitted to a Convention of Delegates, chosen in each State by the People thereof, under the recommendation of its Legislature, for their assent and ratification; and that each Convention assenting to, and ratifying the same, should give Notice thereof to the United States in Congress assembled.

Resolved, That it is the opinion of this Constitution, that as soon as the Conventions of nine States shall have ratified this Constitution, the United States in Congress assembled should fix a day on which Electors should be appointed by the States which shall have ratified the same, and a day on which the Electors should assemble to vote for the President, and the time and place for commencing proceedings under this Constitution. That after such publication the Electors should be appointed, and the Senators and Representatives elected: That the Electors should meet on the day fixed for the Election of the President, and should transmit their votes certified, signed, sealed and directed, as the Constitution requires, to the Secretary of the United States in Congress assembled, that the Senators and Representatives should convene at the time and place assigned; that the Senators should appoint a President of the Senate, for the sole purpose of receiving, opening and counting the votes for President; and, that after he shall be chosen, the Congress, together with the President, should, without delay, proceed to execute this Constitution.

By the unanimous Order of the Convention,
George Washington,
President.
William Jackson, Secretary.

George Washington's Presentation to Congress

In Convention, September 17, 1787.

SIR,

We have now the honor to submit to the consideration of the United States in Congress assembled, that Constitution which has appeared to us the most advisable.

The friends of our country have long seen and desired, that the power of making war, peace and treaties, that of levying money and regulating commerce, and the correspondent executive and judicial authorities should be fully and effectually vested in the general government of the Union: but the impropriety of delegating such extensive trust to one body of men is evident--Hence results the necessity of a different organization.

It is obviously impracticable in the federal government of these States, to secure all rights of independent sovereignty to each, and yet provide for the interest and safety of all--Individuals entering into society, must give up a share of liberty to preserve the rest. The magnitude of the sacrifice must depend as well on situation and circumstance, as on the object to be obtained. It is at all times difficult to draw with precision the line between those rights which must be surrendered, and those which may be reserved; and on the present occasion this difficulty was increased by a difference among the several States as to their situation, extent, habits, and particular interests.

In all our deliberations on this subject we kept steadily in our view, that which appears to us the greatest of every true American, the consolidation of our Union, in which is involved our prosperity, felicity, safety, perhaps our national existence. This important consideration, seriously and deeply impressed on our minds, led each State in the Convention to be less rigid on points of inferior magnitude, than might have been otherwise expected; and thus the Constitution, which we now present, is the result of a spirit of amity, and of that mutual deference and concession which the peculiarity of our political situation rendered indispensable.

That it will meet the full and entire approbation of every State is not perhaps to be expected; but each will doubtless consider, that had her interests been alone consulted, the consequences might have been particularly disagreeable or injurious to others; that it is liable to as few exceptions as could reasonable have been expected, we hope and believe; that it may promote the lasting welfare of that country so dear to us all, and secure her freedom and happiness, is our most ardent wish.

With great respect,
We have the honor to be,
SIR,
Your **Excellency's** most
Obedient and humble Servants,
George Washington, President.
By unanimous Order of the Convention.
HIS EXCELLENCY
The President of Congress.

THE BILL OF RIGHTS

The Bill of Rights

First Ten Amendments to the Constitution

Article I. Congress shall make no law respecting an establishment of religion, or prohibiting the free exercise thereof; or abridging the freedom of speech, or of the press; or the right of the people peaceably to assemble, and to petition the Government for a redress of grievances.

Article II. A well-regulated militia, being necessary to the security of a free state, the right of the people to keep and bear arms, shall not be infringed.

Article III. No soldier shall, in time of peace, be quartered in any house, without the consent of the owner, nor in time of war, but in a manner to be prescribed by law.

Article IV. The right of the people to be secure in their persons, houses, papers, and effects, against unreasonable searches and seizures shall not be violated, and no warrants shall issue, but upon probable cause, supported by oath or affirmation, and particularly describing the place to be searched, and the persons or things to be seized.

Article V. No person shall be held to answer for a capital, or otherwise infamous crime, unless on a presentment or indictment of a grand jury, except in cases arising in the land or naval forces, or in the militia, when in actual service in time of war or public danger; nor shall any person be subject for the same offense to be twice put in jeopardy of life or limb; nor shall be compelled in any criminal case to be a witness against himself, nor be deprived of life, liberty, or property, without due process of law; nor shall private property be taken for public use, without just compensation.

Article VI. In all criminal prosecutions the accused shall enjoy the right to a speedy and public trial, by an impartial jury of the state and district wherein the crime shall have been committed, which district shall have been previously ascertained by law, and to be informed of the nature and cause of the accusation; to be confronted with the witnesses against him; to have compulsory process for obtaining witnesses in his favor, and to have the assistance of counsel for his defense.

Article VII. In suits at common law, where the value in controversy shall exceed twenty dollars, the right of trial by jury shall be preserved, and no fact tried by a jury shall be otherwise re-examined in any court of the United States, than according to the rules of the common law.

Article VIII. Excessive bail shall not be required, nor excessive fines imposed, nor cruel and unusual punishments inflicted.

Article IX. The enumeration in the Constitution, of certain rights, shall not be construed to deny or disparage others retained by the people.

Article X. The powers not delegated to the United States by the Constitution, nor prohibited by it to the states, are reserved to the states respectively, or to the people.

Illuminated Bill of Rights--First ten Articles
(source unknown)

Articles in addition to, and Amendment of the Constitution of the United States of America, proposed by Congress, and ratified by Legislatures of the several States, pursuant to the fifth Article of the original Constitution.

ARTICLE [I]

Congress shall make no law respecting an establishment of religion, or prohibiting the free exercise thereof; or abridging the freedom of speech, or of the press; or the right of the people peaceably to assemble, and to petition the Government for a redress of grievances.

ARTICLE [II]

A well regulated Militia, being necessary to the security of a free State, the right of the people to keep and bear Arms, shall not be infringed.

ARTICLE [III]

No soldier shall, in time of peace be quartered in any house, without the consent of the Owner, nor in time of war, but in a manner to be prescribed by law.

ARTICLE [IV]

The right of the people to be secure in their persons, houses, papers, and effects, against unreasonable searches and seizures, shall not be violated, and no Warrants shall issue, but upon probable cause, supported by Oath or affirmation, and particularly describing the place to be searched, and the persons or things to be seized.

ARTICLE [V]

No person shall be held to answer for capital, or otherwise infamous crime, unless on a presentment or indictment of a Grand Jury, except in cases arising in the land or naval forces, or in the Militia, when in actual service in time of War or public danger; nor shall any person be subject for the same offence to be twice put in jeopardy of life or limb; nor shall be compelled in any criminal case to be a witness against himself, nor be deprived of life, or property, without due process of law; nor shall private property be taken for public use, without just compensation.

ARTICLE [VI]

In all criminal prosecutions, the accused shall enjoy the right to a speedy and public trial, by an impartial jury of the State and district wherein the crime shall have been committed, which district shall have been previously ascertained by law, and to be informed of the nature and cause of the accusation; to be confronted with the witnesses against him; to have compulsory process for obtaining witnesses in his favor, and to have the Assistance of Counsel for his defence.

ARTICLE [VII]

In Suits at common law, where the value in controversy shall exceed twenty dollars, the right of trial by jury shall be preserved, and no fact tried by a jury, shall be otherwise re-examined in any Court of the United States, than according to the rules of the common law.

ARTICLE [VIII]

Excessive bail shall not be required, nor excessive fines imposed, nor cruel and unusual punishments inflicted.

ARTICLE [IX]

The enumeration in the Constitution, of certain rights, shall not be construed to deny or disparage others retained by the people.

ARTICLE [X]

The powers not delegated to the United States by the Constitution, nor prohibited by it to the States, are reserved to the States respectively, or to the people.

AMENDMENTS

ARTICLE [XI]

The Judicial power of the United States shall not be construed to extend to any suit in law or equity, commenced or prosecuted against one of the United States by Citizens of another State, or by the Citizens or Subjects of any Foreign State.

ARTICLE [XII]

The Electors shall meet in their respective states, and vote by ballot for President and Vice-President, one of whom, at least, shall not be an inhabitant of the same state with themselves; they shall name in their ballots the person voted for as President, and in distinct ballots the person voted for as Vice-President, and they shall make distinct lists of all persons voted for as President, and of all persons voted for as Vice-President, and of the number of votes for each, which lists they shall sign and certify, and transmit sealed to the seat of the government of the United States, directed to the President of the Senate;--The President of the Senate shall, in the presence of the Senate and House of Representatives, open all the certificates and the votes shall then be counted;--The person having the greatest number of votes for President, if such number be a majority of the whole number of Electors appointed; and if no person have such majority, then from the persons having the highest numbers not exceeding three on the list of those voted for as President, the House of Representatives shall choose immediately, by ballot, the President. But in choosing the President, the votes shall be taken by states, the representation from each state having one vote; a quorum for this purpose shall consist of a member or members from two-thirds of the states, and a majority of all the states shall be necessary to a choice. [And if the House of Representatives shall not choose a President whenever the right of choice shall devolve upon them, before the fourth day of March next following, then the Vice-President shall act as President, as in the case of the death or other constitutional disability of the President.] *(The part enclosed in brackets has been superseded by section 3 of Amendment XX.)* The person having the greatest number of votes as Vice-President, shall be the Vice-President, if such number be a majority of the whole number of Electors appointed, and if no person have a majority, then from the two highest numbers on the list, the Senate shall choose the Vice-President; a quorum for the purpose shall consist of two-thirds of the whole number of Senators, and a majority of the whole number shall be necessary to a choice. But no person constitutionally ineligible to the office of President shall be eligible to that of Vice-President of the United States.

ARTICLE [XIII]

Section 1. Neither slavery nor involuntary servitude, except as a punishment for crime whereof the party shall have been duly convicted, shall exist within the United States, or any place subject to their jurisdiction.

Section 2. Congress shall have power to enforce this article by appropriate legislation.

ARTICLE [XIV]

Section 1. All persons born or naturalized in the United States, and subject to the jurisdiction thereof, are citizens of the United States and of the State wherein they reside. No State shall make or enforce any law which shall abridge the privileges or immunities of citizens of the United States; nor shall any State deprive any person of life, liberty, or property, without due process of law; nor deny to any person within its jurisdiction the equal protection of the laws.

Section 2. Representatives shall be apportioned among the several States according to their respective numbers, counting the whole number of persons in each State, excluding Indians not taxed. But when the right to vote at any election for the choice of electors for President and Vice President of the United States, Representatives in Congress, the Executive and Judicial officers of a State, or the members of the Legislature thereof, is denied to any of the male inhabitants of such State, being twenty-one years of age, and citizens of the United States, or in any way abridged, except for participation in rebellion, or other crimes, the basis of representation therein shall be reduced in the proportion which the number of such male citizens shall bear to the whole number of male citizens twenty-one years of age in such State.

Section 3. No person shall be a Senator or Representative in Congress, or elector of President and Vice President, or hold any office, civil or military, under the United States, or under any State, who, having previously taken an oath, as a member of Congress, or as an officer of the United States, or as a member of any State legislature, or as an executive or judicial officer of any State, to support the Constitution of the United States, shall have engaged in insurrection or rebellion against the same, or given aid or comfort to the enemies thereof. But Congress may by a vote of two-thirds of each House, remove such disability.

Section 4. The validity of the public debt of the United States, authorized by law, including debts incurred for payment of pensions and bounties for services in suppressing insurrection or rebellion, shall not be questioned. But neither the United States nor any State shall assume or pay any debt or obligation incurred in aid of insurrection or rebellion against the United States, or any claim for the loss or emancipation of any slave; but all such debts, obligations and claims shall be held illegal and void.

Section 5. The Congress shall have power to enforce, by appropriate legislation, the provisions of this article.

ARTICLE [XV]

Section 1. The right of citizens of the United States to vote shall not be denied or abridged by the United States or by any State on account of race, color, or previous condition of servitude.

Section 2. The Congress shall have the power to enforce this article by appropriate legislation.

ARTICLE [XVI]

The Congress shall have power to lay and collect taxes on incomes, from whatever source derived, without apportionment among the several States, and without regard to any census or enumeration.

ARTICLE [XVII]

The Senate of the United States shall be composed of two Senators from each State, elected by the people thereof, for six years; and each Senator shall have one vote. The electors in each State shall have the qualifications requisite for electors of the most numerous branch of the State legislatures.

When vacancies happen in the representation of any State in the Senate, the executive authority of such State shall issue writs of election to fill such vacancies: *Provided*, That the legislature of any State may empower the executive thereof to make temporary appointments until the people fill the vacancies by election as the legislature may direct.

This amendment shall not be so construed as to affect the election or term of any Senator chosen before it becomes valid as part of the Constitution.

ARTICLE [XVIII]

Section 1. After one year from the ratification of this article the manufacture, sale, or transportation of intoxicating liquors within, the importation thereof into, or the exportation thereof from the United States and all territory subject to the jurisdiction thereof for beverage purposes is hereby prohibited.

Section 2. The Congress and the several States shall have concurrent power to enforce this article by appropriate legislation.

Section 3. This article shall be inoperative unless it shall have been ratified as an amendment to the Constitution by the legislatures of the several States, as provided in the Constitution, within seven years from the date of the submission hereof to the submission hereof to the States by Congress. *(Repealed in 1933).*

ARTICLE [XIX]

The right of citizens of the United States to vote shall not be denied or abridged by the United States or by any State on account of sex.

Congress shall have power to enforce this article by appropriate legislation.

ARTICLE [XX]

Section 1. The terms of the President and Vice President shall end at noon on the 20th day of January, and the terms of Senators and Representatives at noon on the 3rd day of January, of the years in which such terms would have ended if this article had not been ratified; and the terms of their successors shall then begin.

Section 2. The Congress shall assemble at least once in every year, and such meeting shall begin at noon on the 3rd day of January, unless they shall by law appoint a different day.

Section 3. If, at the time fixed for the beginning of the term of the President, the President elect shall have died, the Vice President elect shall become President. If a President shall not have been chosen before the time fixed for the beginning of his term, or if the President elect shall have failed to qualify, then the Vice President elect shall act as President until a President shall have qualified; and the Congress may by law provide for the case wherein neither a President elect nor a Vice President elect shall have qualified, declaring who shall then act as President, or the manner in which one who is to act shall be selected, and such person shall act accordingly until a President or Vice President shall have qualified.

Section 4. The Congress may by law provide for the case of the death of any persons from whom the House of Representatives may choose a President whenever the right of choice shall have devolved upon them, and for the case of the death of any of the persons from whom the Senate may choose a Vice President whenever the right of choice shall have devolved upon them.

Section 5. Section 1 and 2 shall take effect on the 15th day of October following the ratification of this article.

Section 6. This article shall be inoperative unless it shall have been ratified as an amendment to the Constitution by the legislatures of three-fourths of the several States within seven years from the date of its submission.

ARTICLE [XXI]

Section 1. The eighteenth article of amendment to the Constitution of the United States is hereby repealed.

Section 2. The transportation or importation into any State, Territory, or possession of the United States for delivery or use therein of intoxicating liquors, in violation of the laws thereof, is hereby prohibited.

Section 3. This article shall be inoperative unless it shall have been ratified as an amendment to the Constitution by conventions in the several States, as provided in the Constitution, within seven years from the date of the submission hereof to the States by the Congress.

ARTICLE [XXII]

Section 1. No person shall be elected to the office of the President more than twice, and no person who has held the office of President, or acted as President, for more than two years of a term to which some other person was elected President shall be elected to the office of the President more than once. But this Article shall not apply to any person holding the office of President when this Article was proposed by the Congress, and shall not prevent any person who may be holding the office of President, or acting as President, during the term within which this Article becomes operative from holding the office of President or acting as President during the remainder of such term.

Section 2. This article shall be inoperative unless it shall have been ratified as an amendment to the Constitution by the legislatures of three-fourths of the several States within seven years from the date of its submission to the States by the Congress.

ARTICLE [XXIII]

Section 1. The District constituting the seat of Government of the United States shall appoint in such manner as the Congress may direct:

A number of electors of President and Vice President equal to the whole number of Senators and Representatives in Congress to which the District would be entitled if it were a State, but in no event more than the least populous State; they shall be in addition to those appointed by the States, but they shall be considered, for the purposes of the election of President and Vice President, to be electors appointed by a State; and they shall meet in the District and perform such duties as provided by the twelfth article of amendment.

Section 2. The Congress shall have power to enforce this article by appropriate legislation.

ARTICLE [XXIV]

Section 1. The right of citizens of the United States to vote in any primary or other election for President or Vice President, for electors for President or Vice President, or for Senator or Representative in Congress, shall not be denied or abridged by the United States or any State by reason of failure to pay any poll tax or other tax.

Section 2. The Congress shall have power to enforce this article by appropriate legislation.

ARTICLE [XXV]

Section 1. In case of the removal of the President from office or of his death or resignation, the Vice President shall become President.

Section 2. Whenever there is a vacancy in the office of the Vice President, the President shall nominate a Vice President who shall take office upon confirmation by a majority vote of both Houses of Congress.

Section 3. Whenever the President transmits to the President pro tempore of the Senate and the Speaker of the House of Representatives his written declaration that he is unable to discharge the powers and duties of his office, and until he transmits to them a written declaration to the contrary, such powers and duties shall be discharged by the Vice President as Acting President.

Section 4. Whenever the Vice President and a majority of either the principal officers of the executive departments or of such other body as Congress may by law provide, transmit to the President pro tempore of the Senate and the Speaker of the House of Representatives their written declaration that the President is unable to discharge the powers and duties of his office, the Vice President shall immediately assume the powers and duties of the office as Acting President.

Thereafter, when the President transmits to the President pro tempore of the Senate and the Speaker of the House of Representatives his written declaration that no inability exists, he shall resume the powers and duties of his office unless the Vice President and a majority of either the principal officers of the executive department or of such other body as Congress may by law provide, transmit within four days to the President pro tempore of the Senate and the Speaker of the House of Representatives their written declaration that the President is unable to discharge the powers and duties of his office. Thereupon Congress shall decide the issue, assembling within forty-eight hours for that purpose if not in session. If the Congress, within twenty-one days after receipt of the latter written declaration, or, if congress is not in session, within twenty-one days after Congress is required to assemble, determines by two-thirds vote of both Houses that the President is unable to discharge the powers and duties of his office, the Vice President shall continue to discharge the same as Acting President; otherwise, the President shall resume the powers and duties of his office.

ARTICLE [XXVI]

ection 1. The right of citizens of the United States, who are eighteen years of age or older, to vote shall not be

S

denied or abridged by the United States or by any State on account of age.

Section 2. The Congress shall have power to enforce this article by appropriate legislation.

EMANCIPATION PROCLAMATION

EMANCIPATION PROCLAMATION
1863

Whereas, on the twenty-second day of September, in the year of our Lord one thousand eight hundred and sixty-two, a proclamation was issued by the President of the United States, containing, among other things, the following, to wit:

> That on the first day of January, in the year of our Lord one thousand eight hundred and sixty-three, all persons held as slaves within any State, or designated part of a State, the people whereof shall then be in rebellion against the United States, shall be then, thenceforward, and forever free; and the Executive Government of the United States, including the military and naval authority thereof, will recognize and maintain the freedom of such persons, and will do no act or acts to repress such persons, or any of them, in any efforts they may make for their actual freedom.
>
> That the Executive will, on the first day of January aforesaid, by proclamation, designate the States and parts of States, if any, in which the people thereof respectively, shall then be in

rebellion against the United States; and the fact that any State, or the people thereof, shall on that day be in good faith represented in the Congress of the United States by members chosen thereto at elections wherein a majority of the qualified voters of such State shall have participated, shall in the absence of strong countervailing testimony, be deemed conclusive evidence that such State, and the people thereof, are not then in rebellion against the United States.

Now, therefore, I, Abraham Lincoln, President of the United States, by virtue of the power in me vested as commander-in-chief of the Army and Navy of the United States, in time of actual armed rebellion against authority and government of the United States, and as a fit and necessary war measure for suppressing said rebellion, do, on this first day of January, in the year of our Lord one thousand eight hundred and sixty-three, and in accordance with my purpose so to do, publicly proclaimed for the full period of one hundred days from the day first above mentioned, order and designate as the States and parts of States wherein the people thereof, respectively, are this day in rebellion against the United States, the following, to wit:

Arkansas, Texas, Louisiana (except the parishes of St. Bernard, Plaquemines, Jefferson, St. John, St. Charles, St. James, Ascension, Assumption, Terrebonne, Lafourche, St. Mary, St. Martin, and Orleans, including the city of New Orleans), Mississippi, Alabama, Florida, Georgia, South Carolina, North Carolina, and

Virginia (except the forty-eight counties designated as West Virginia, and also the counties of Berkley, Accomac, Northampton, Elizabeth City, York, Princess Ann, and Norfolk, including the cities of Norfolk and Portsmouth), and which excepted parts are, for the present, left precisely as if this proclamation were not issued.

And by virtue of the power and for the purpose aforesaid, I do order and declare that all persons held as slaves within said designated States and parts of States are, and henceforward shall be, free; and that the Executive government of the United States, including the military and naval authorities thereof, will recognize and maintain the freedom of said persons.

And I hereby enjoin upon the people so declared to be free to abstain from all violence, unless in necessary self-defence; and I recommend to them that, in all cases when allowed, they labor faithfully for reasonable wages.

And I further declare and make known, that such persons of suitable condition, will be received into the armed service of the United States to garrison forts, positions, stations, and other places, and to man vessels of all sorts in said service.

And upon this act, sincerely believed to be an act of justice, warranted by the Constitution, upon military necessity, I invoke the considerate judgment of mankind and the gracious favor of Almighty God.

In witness whereof, I have hereunto set my hand, and caused the seal of the United States to be affixed.

Done at the city of Washington, this first day of January, in the year of our Lord one thousand eight hundred and sixty-three, and of the Independence of the United States of America the eighty-seventh.

ABRAHAM LINCOLN.

WILLIAM H. SEWARD, Secretary of State.

PROMISSORY NOTE

PROMISSORY NOTE

"I have a dream" speech
by Martin Luther King, Jr.

In a sense we have come to the capital to cash a check. When the architects of our republic wrote the magnificent words of the Constitution and the Declaration of Independence, they were signing a promissory note to which every American was to fall heir. This note was a promise that all men--black men as well as white men--would be guaranteed the inalienable rights of life, liberty, and the pursuit of happiness.

But it is obvious that America has defaulted on this promissory note insofar as her citizens of color are concerned. Instead of honoring this sacred obligation, America has given the Negro people a bad check--a check that has come back marked "insufficient funds." But we refuse to believe that the bank of justice is bankrupt. We refuse to believe that there are insufficient funds in the great vaults of opportunity in this Nation.

So we have come to cash this check. A check that will give us the riches of freedom and the security of justice.

We have also come to this hallowed spot to remind America that the fierce urgency is now. This is no time to engage in the luxury of cooling off or to take the tranquilizing drug of gradualism. Now is the time to make real the promise of democracy. Now is the time to rise from the dark and desolate valley of segregation to the sunlit path of racial justice. Now is the time to lift our Nation from the quicksands of racial injustice to the solid rock of brotherhood. Now is the time to make justice a reality for all of God's children.

Those who hope that the Negro needed to blow off steam and will be content will have a rude awakening if the Nation returns to business as usual. There will be neither rest nor tranquillity in America until the Negro is granted his citizenship rights. The whirlwind of revolt will continue to shake the foundations of our Nation until the bright day of Justice emerges.

But there is something that I must say to my people who stand on the warm threshold which leads into the palace of Justice. In the process of gaining our rightful place, we must not be guilty of wrongful deeds. Let us not seek to satisfy our thirst for freedom by drinking from the cup of bitterness and hatred.

We must forever continue our struggle on the high plane of dignity and discipline. We must not allow our creative protest to degenerate into physical violence. Again and again we must rise to the majestic heights of meeting physical force with soul force.

The marvelous new militancy which has engulfed the Negro community must not lead us to a distrust of all white people--for many or our white brothers, as evidenced by their presence here today, have come to realize that their destiny is inextricably tied up with our destiny. They have come to realize that their freedom is inextricably bound to our freedom.

We cannot walk alone, and as we walk, we must make the pledge that we shall always march ahead. We cannot turn back. There are those who are asking the devotees of civil rights: "When will you be satisfied?" We can never be satisfied as long as the Negro is the victim of unspeakable horrors of police brutality. We can never be satisfied as long as our bodies, heavy with the fatigue of travel, cannot gain lodging in the motels of the highways and the hotels of the cities. We can never be satisfied as long as the Negro's basic mobility is from a smaller ghetto to a larger one. We can never be satisfied as long as our children are stripped of their selfhood and robbed of their dignity by signs stating "For Whites Only."

I have a dream that my four little children will one day live in a Nation where they will not be judged by the color of their skins, but by the conduct of their character.

I have a dream that one day in Alabama, with this vicious racist, its Governor, having his lips dripping the words of interposition and nullification--one day right here in Alabama, little black boys and black girls will be able to join hands with little white boys and little white girls as brothers and sisters.

I have a dream that one day every valley shall be exalted: every hill and mountain shall be made low, the rough places will be made plane, the crooked places will be made straight and the glory of the Lord shall be revealed and all flesh shall see it together.

BECCARIA IN THE AMERICAN EXPERIENCE

THE DECLARATION OF CAUSES... and Mazzei

During the 1770 decade, aside from the English-speaking colonists, there were also the Dutch in the New York area, the French in Canada and Louisiana, the Germans in the Pennsylvania area, the Spaniards in the California, Florida, Central an South American areas, and the Portuguese in Brazil. The Declaration of Causes, however, was written, printed and published in English, and translated but never printed or published in Italian.

Its Italian rendition is to be found in the Library of Congress as part of the Jefferson papers. The question is why an Italian version, when in the colonies there was neither an Italian-speaking community, nor a hegemonic government in Italy. The search for an answer to that question gave several surprising results.

Italians made some rather important contributions toward the establishment of America's democratic form of government. Documents and other correspondence show the Italians, directly and indirectly, played active roles in the English-speaking colonies.

In a letter to Philip Mazzei, Benjamin Franklin expresses his delight over the fact that Mazzei (upon receiving a copy of the 1775 Declaration of Causes directly from and in the handwriting of Thomas Jefferson himself), had made a translation into Italian and sent a copy to the Duke of Tuscany.

That Mazzei had made a translation of the final rendition of the 1775 Declaration may be of little importance in itself. That he should have received a copy directly from Jefferson may be explained by the fact that Mazzei and Jefferson had been and were good friends. More than this, since Mazzei had written many articles and pamphlets on behalf of independence for America, and because he may have been more influential in stirring the colonists against the English tyranny than is otherwise known, Jefferson may have wanted to express his appreciation to Mazzei by sending him a personal copy.

Philip Mazzei, who went to Virginia by way of England in the late months of 1773 together with a Mrs. Martin and her daughter (whom Mazzei regretfully married at a later date), held many important positions from the time of his arrival to the time he returned to Europe in the fall of 1778 as an envoy of the State of Virginia with the purpose of raising funds and gaining support for the united colonies. This mission had been projected in the Declaration of Causes: "Our cause is just. Our union is perfect. Our internal resources are great, and if necessary foreign assistance is undoubtedly attainable."

From 1773 to 1778, a most crucial period for the colonies, Mazzei became an elected official of the vestry. Commercially, he formed a company for the purpose of making wine and oil, and of introducing to the continent vines and other agricultural plants and silk. As a soldier, he joined the Independent Company of Albermale, fighting against the British on behalf of Virginia, all the while writing articles and pamphlets under the pen-name of *Furioso* during the years 1774-75 and publishing them in John Pinkney's *Virginia Gazette* (Mazzei, *Memoirs*, translation by H.R. Marraro, Columbia U. Press, N.Y. 1942).

This Italian traveler and adventurer went from Italy to Smyrna, to England, to North America, to Poland, and to various other European countries and back to North America and finally back to Italy, then to Poland, and to Russia. In America, he counted personal friends such as John, Richard and Thomas Adams, Carlo Bellini, Benjamin Franklin, Patrick Henry, Lafayette, Thomas Jefferson, James Madison and George Washington to name a few; America's first five elected presidents corresponded with him: Washington, Adams, Jefferson, Madison and Monroe.

As happened to his many American counterparts, on reading *On Crimes and Punishments*, Mazzei quickly espoused Beccaria's utilitarian philosophy of the "felicità pubblica" (maximum happiness to the greatest number of people). He made it clear that he was as much against pedigree hegemonies as he was against the establishment of religious monopolies such as state churches, especially if backed by established governments. Together with Jefferson, Madison, and John Adams, Mazzei directly and indirectly reduced Beccaria's "humane and wise treatise" to a system of laws that found their practical framework in documents like the declarations of Causes and of Independence, and the Constitution of the United States of America with its Beccarian Bill of Rights.

During the crucial years of 1774-75 that saw the shaping process for what was going to be a future American independent nation, in John Pinkney's *Gazette*, Mazzei wrote the following:

> To attain our goal it is necessary, my dear fellow-citizens, to discuss the natural rights of man and the foundations of a free government ... All men are by nature free and independent. This equality is essential to the establishment of a liberal government. Every individual must be equal to every other in his natural rights. The division of society into ranks has always been and will always continue to be a very serious obstacle to the attainment of this end... I repeat that a truly republican form of government cannot exist except where all men--from the very rich to the very poor--are perfectly equal in their natural rights. Fortunately, we are now free on this continent... Now when certain privileges are exercised by a portion of the inhabitants and denied to others, it is vain to hope for the establishment of a liberal and permanent government, unless the favored citizens are willing to relinquish their privileges and stand on a footing of perfect equality with the rest of the inhabitants. Discrimination inevitably arouses envy and ill-feeling... Therefore, liberty will always be insecure and finally doomed to collapse... Democracy, I mean representative democracy, which embraces all individuals in one simple body, without any distinction whatsoever, is certainly the only form of government under which a true and enduring liberty may be

> enjoyed. Unfortunately for mankind, this form of government has never existed. The sacred name of democracy has been abused by tumultuous governments built on false and unstable principles... (from his *Memoirs*).

Much of Mazzei's work during this time involved research on the body of laws that comprise the Constitution of England (there not being a single document as such, however) with the goal of finding out its many defects. But perhaps the greatest lesson he imparted to the colonists was the Beccarian observation that enslavement of the mind on the part of certain groups (political, religious, etc) can easily be accomplished through various brainwashing techniques.

In his *Memoirs*, Mazzei reveals that even "Jefferson was amazed at the defects of the English form of government when I pointed them out to him, saying that they had not even occurred to him."

Pursuant to Jefferson's admission, Mazzei goes on to explain why this had taken place and could still take place:

> Ever since childhood, you have heard that it was the best possible type of government: you could see that it was such, in comparison with the other governments of Europe; you must have read English authors who proved that it is far better than that of the Roman republic; finally, never dreaming of having to change it, you lacked the incentive to examine it in detail. But, provoked by the insolent way in which the English express themselves about other nations--'They are 400 years behind the times'--,

> I have examined it carefully and have noted the essential defects I have described to you. (*Memoirs*, p. 204)

To this, Jefferson suggested that Mazzei go on with the research and publish his findings in the form of articles in order to bring "these defects to the attention of everyone." (See *Camillus* at end of this chapter).

In the mind of Mazzei, however, publishing the findings was not enough. The newly discovered information had to be used to encourage and stimulate discussions among the people so as "to combat the prevailing prejudices and to point out saner principles." To this end, Mazzei diligently set about to engage in discussions with the goal of bringing out the "saner principles."

The "saner principles" involved political and religious activities. The latter, in fact, was of paramount importance, knowing well, as did Beccaria, that even the smallest religious jealousies could precipitate the type of dissension which would weaken the bonds of a constituted society and play into the hands of the enemy. Without losing sight of the various practices of religious sects, and with complete tolerance for the faith of others, Mazzei made himself the watchdog against those who preached dependence on England and used religious power and pulpits as means toward this end.

On being aware of this danger, Jefferson asked Mazzei to help. "Jefferson sought my opinion on many matters," Mazzei says in his *Memoirs*, and among the many matters, the most important was the religious issue, especially that which dealt with certain special rights reserved to the predominant Anglican denomination.

> Its ministers could not bear being placed on an equal footing with those of other denominations and reduced to living on the voluntary contributions of their parishioners, after having been supported until then by the state. (*Memoirs*, p. 215)

Edmund Pendleton attempted to discredit Mazzei by fabricating false accusations which he then secretly "leaked" to the press and to the people. Mazzei was accused of "wishing to introduce popery" into the colonies. On discovering the plot, Jefferson answered by saying, "Pendleton will see that the shoe fits him."

On another occasion, Mazzei went to hear a Methodist from England preaching on behalf of the status quo:

> When we arrived, he had been speaking of the dangers which beset the soul through sudden death; then he mentioned how great that danger was in time of war and recalled to the minds of mothers and fathers their duty toward their children, namely, to remove them from danger.
>
> One could easily see the point of his sermon. As soon as he had descended from the pulpit, I ascended it and told him that, having listened to his evangelical doctrine, I hoped he would be so kind as to listen to mine. Although he said not a word, he showed that he was anxious to leave, but my friends told him in an authoritative manner that he must stay.
>
> I began by saying that the intention of the British government was made clearly manifest

> by the Boston blockade, by armed encounter which had taken place on the outskirts of that city, by our governor's conduct, by the landing of English troops at Hampton, and so on.
>
> Then I spoke of Lord Dartmouth, who had been made secretary of state, so that he might send his satellites to the colonies to preach the doctrine which we had heard from that minister, and by means of which our adversaries hoped to place a yoke around our necks, without the least opposition. But I predicted (turning to him) that they would make the trip in vain. (*Memoirs*, pp. 216-7)

It may be opportune to mention that upon leaving Virginia in 1779 on his mission to Europe, Mazzei took with him the following documents: Bill for Establishing Religious Freedom, Bill on Crimes and Punishments, Bill on the Qualifications Requisite to Constitute a Citizen, and two bills on Public Establishment for Education.

In his *Declaration of Independence: Its History* (Dodd, Mead & Co.), N.Y. 1906, Hazelton published this interesting comparison of how similar rights were handled in England and in America, written by *Camillus*, the pen-name used by several individuals during this period. Camillus, the second founder of the Roman Empire after Romulus and Remus, was also considered the father of his country. Around 365 B.C., he conquered the Etruscans, and gave Rome a new code of laws. Because of special interest groups, he often found himself clashing with countrymen over issues on how to govern.

ENGLAND

1. A trial by a jury of his country, in all cases of life and property.

2. A trial where the offence was committed.

3. A civil authority supreme over the military, and no standing army in time of peace kept up, but by the consent of the people.

4. The judges independent of the Crown and people.

5. No tax or imposition laid, but by those who must partake of the burthen.

6. A free trade to all the world, except the East-Indies.

7. A free use and practice of all engines and other devices, for saving labour and promoting manufacturers.

8. A right to petition the King, and all prosecutions and commitments therefor illegal.

9. Freedom of debate and proceedings in their legislative deliberations.

10. For redress of grievances, amending, strengthening and preserving the laws, parliaments to be held frequently.

AMERICA

1. A Trial by jury only in some cases, subjected in others to a single judge, or a Board of Commissioners.

2. A trial, if a governor pleases, 3000 miles from the place where the offence was committed.

3. The military superior to the civil authority, and America obliged to contribute to the

support of a standing army, kept up without and against its consent.

4. The judges made independent of the people, but dependent on the Crown for the support and tenure of their commissions.

5. Taxes and impositions laid by those, who not only do not partake of the burthens, but who ease themselves by it.

6. A trade only to such places as Great-Britain shall permit.

7. The use only of such engines as Great-Britain has not prohibited.

8. Promoting and encouraging petitions to the King declared the highest presumption, and the legislative assemblies of America dissolved therefore in 1768.

9. Assemblies dissolved, their legislative power suspended, for the free exercise of their reason and judgement, in their legislative capacity.

10. To prevent the redress of grievances, or representations tending thereto, assemblies postponed for a great length of time, and prevented meeting in the most critical times.

CESARE BECCARIA

AN
ESSAY
ON
CRIMES
AND
PUNISHMENTS.

WRITTEN BY THE
MARQUIS BECCARIA,
OF MILAN.

WITH A
COMMENTARY,
Attributed to Monsieur De VOLTAIRE.

In the present age, we seem universally aiming at perfection; let us not therefore forget to perfect the LAWS, on which our LIVES and FORTUNES depend. *Voltaire.*

Wherever truth and interest shall embrace,
Let passion cool, and prejudice give place. *Brooke.*

PHILADELPHIA:
Printed and Sold by R. BELL, next Door to St. Paul's Church, in Third-Street.
M.DCC.LXXVIII.

AN
ESSAY
ON
CRIMES
AND
PUNISHMENTS
Translated from the ITALIAN;
WITH A
COMMENTARY,
Attributed to Mons. DE VOLTAIRE.
Translated from the FRENCH.

In rebus quibuscumque difficilioribus non expectandum, ut quis simul, & serat, & metat, sed praeparatione opus est, ut per gradus maturescant. BACON.

STATE OF SOUTH CAROLINA.
PRINTED AND SOLD BY DAVID BRUCE, AT HIS SHOP IN CHURCH-STREET, CHARLESTOWN.
M DCC LXXVII.

BECCARIA

America's Spiritual Founding Father

Cesare Beccaria's treatise, *On Crimes and Punishments*, was so influential that many nations of Europe changed parts of their constitutions while the author was still alive.

In an America of the revolutionary period, the book was more influential than any other single book, its spirit incorporated in documents such as the Declaration of Causes, the Declaration of Independence, the Constitution, and the Bill of Rights.

John Adams quoted from it as early as 1768; later, the same Adams quoted Beccaria in both English and Italian. Thomas Jefferson made extensive usage of the book, as did many other prominent Americans of the same period.

It may be a surprise to many students and scholars alike in discovering that Beccaria's book was published in America long before any book of men such as Voltaire, Rousseau, and Montesquieu, to name just a few.

With the help of this book, our American forefathers were able to resolve issues such as the separation of church and state, the role of organized religions, the type and role of government, the role of the citizen, and of the Federation. Yet, many issues raised by Beccaria are still unresolved. The religious issue, capital punishment, secret accusations, and many others are being discussed all over America.

In reading the old English translation of *On Crimes and Punishments*, we might re-discover another dimension of the 1770 decade as well as find answers or solutions to problems that are pressing us, our society and our government.

That this prominent jurist from Milan played an important role in the development of the documents that constitute America's Democracy has been a fact overlooked by such historians as Becker, Hazelton, Kimball, and Bailyn.

BECCARIA

AND THE AMERICAN REVOLUTION

Beccaria's *Dei Delitti e Delle Pene* (On Crimes and Punishments) may have been the single most influential book of the second half of the eighteenth century, having influenced both Europeans and Americans of the Revolutionary period.

In connection with the American experience, it can be said, without risking too much, that this single book found more outright application in making and shaping the new nation than is otherwise believed. The Declaration of Causes of 1775, the Declaration of Independence of 1776, the Constitution and the Bill of Rights can be traced to Beccaria's book, not so much for that which deals specifically with criminal law, but for that which deals with the basic rights of man, with the relationships that ought to exist between man and man, between man and his society, and between man and his government.

In Beccaria's mind, man was the center of the entire human experience--his motto being: happiness to the greatest number. With the individual citizen placed above all other things, old and new governments had to assure the possibility of allowing the individual to achieve happiness.

In "We, the people...", Beccaria would see it as the law having inherent, automatic and immediate self-implementation, requiring no other law or regulations to be fulfilled.

Were it not for customs in general and the obtuse hearts of far too many men, individuals of both sexes, be they of different racial or religious groups, would only need to cite "We, the people..." to achieve basic equality and the potential of great degrees of happiness according to their personal strengths and desires.

It follows, then, that only through a sound system of laws can the citizen assure himself the potential attainment of happiness. Laws, therefore, have to be made to secure this goal, and those laws which do not accomplish the purpose or abridge unnecessarily the liberty of the citizen must be immediately repealed.

Laws need be written in the simplest language possible so the citizens can read and understand them, and be responsible only for those acts which are specifically stated by those laws.

Lawmakers should look to the future and pass laws according to the needs of changing times, repealing those which have no bearing on present generations. In any event, whenever an individual runs counter to the laws, be the offense civil or criminal, Beccaria upholds the Roman principle which is basic to our system: the individual is innocent until proven guilty, that no individual can be punished or tortured, and no individual can be made to accuse himself in a court of law or in any other place. Furthermore, if an accusation against an individual, of whatever nature, cannot be made public, such accusation has to be considered null and void. Furthermore, accusations have to be corroborated by evidence of fact and not by evidence of hearsay. The latter make possible witchhunts and other similar abominable abuses.

Secret accusations, therefore, are not admissible, nor should they be allowed in a free state. Likewise, capital punishment should not be practiced in a nation that at the same time lays claim to civility and humanity.

Religion, being an individual experience, has to remain such, and free of compromise. It must not come into play as an entity within the structure of government; it must be separate from the government. But, that very government must guarantee and protect the right of the citizen to believe and to practice according to his religious disposition.

Governments that officially adhere to a given religion become, in the eyes of Beccaria, as tyrannical as organized religion, because human nature always aspires to superimpose one's own beliefs and practices on others. To avoid tyranny under the guise of spirituality, Beccaria proclaims separation of church and state, with religion being practiced on an individual or social basis and not as a mandate of the government.

It is not an understatement to say that Beccaria presented to our American Forefathers certain ideas that allowed them to resolve serious problems and to establish a viable form of government. His spirit was very much alive in John Adams, Thomas Jefferson, Thomas Paine, George Washington, Benjamin Franklin, James Wilson, James Madison, and many others. But his spirit is much more alive in the various documents that have established the guidelines for new and old governments, and in books and pamphlets as *Common Sense* and *The Rights of Man*.

JOHN ADAMS AND BECCARIA

One of the first to quote directly from Beccaria's book was John Adams, who, as is commonly held, influenced the course of events of this country as one of its greatest constitutional lawyers.

Together with his cousin Samuel, John Adams signed the Declaration of Independence; was the first Vice President and the second President of the newly-formed nation. In 1791, during his term as Vice-President, he saw the Bill of Rights become part of the Constitution. He was also a member of the Continental Congress from 1774-1778. He was involved, therefore, in practically every important event that led to the shaping of the various documents of the U.S. government, being particularly instrumental in bringing about the Constitution, which as a document, still governs with an effectiveness that has seen no equal.

It is important to note that John Adams concerned himself as much with the rights of the single individual as in assuring to all men the protection of those rights, even if it meant going counter to popular sentiments and against his own interests. This was the conscious and definitive driving force behind John Adams, the same force that permeates the documents on which this country's government is founded.

This spirit may be reflected in the unpopular actions he willingly took in defense of Captain Preston, in connection with the 1770 Boston Massacre.

The roots of Adams' defense are to be found in the case of Rex v. Samuel Quinn, Worcester Superior Court, September 1768, as a result of which "the Man was acquitted."

Some two years after the Worcester decision, during a trip he was taking to Plymouth on Thursday, June 28, 1770, John Adams recalls the trial of 1768: "I have received such Blessings and enjoyed such Tears of Transport--and there is no greater Pleasure, or Consolation!"

The individual responsible for this joyful outburst was Cesare Beccaria from whose book Adams took the passage:

> If, by supporting the Rights of Mankind, and of invincible Truth, I shall contribute to save from the Agonies of Death one unfortunate Victim of Tyranny, or of Ignorance, equally fatal; his Blessing and Tears of Transport, will be sufficient Consolation to me, for the Contempt of all Mankind. (*Essay on Crimes and Punishments*. Page 42. *The Adams Papers* "Diary and Autobiography of John Adams," Vol. I, The Belknap Press, Cambridge, MA, 1961, pp. 352-54.)

Quoting directly from Beccaria in 1770 on an incident that occurred in 1768 means that Adams must have known of Beccaria's book as early as 1768. English editions had appeared in Dublin as early as 1767. What should also be said is that Beccaria's book inspired Adams' action as early as 1770 when he defended Captain Preston, a symbol of what Samuel

Adams called the "horrid Massacre" of Boston, which took place the evening of March 5.

The soldiers of the Twenty-ninth Regiment were alleged to have massacred children, women, and men. To prove the "horrid Massacre", Samuel Adams obtained sworn statements from ninety-six witnesses in support of the prosecutors. In view of these things, and knowing of his cousin's feelings against the English, John Adams, together with Josiah Quincy, accepted to defend Captain Preston and his six soldiers. Aided by the testimony of Patrick Carr, John Adams was able to have Captain Preston and his men acquitted.

In his defense, John Adams frequently made references to the ideas of Beccaria. In his, *The Boston Massacre*, Zobel observes that when John Adams quoted directly from Beccaria, he had an electrifying effect on the jury. The passage that culminated his eloquent defense was the one he had included in his Diary of June 28, 1770.

Obviously, Beccaria did not make just a passing impression on John Adams. As late as July 1786, some 16 years after his defense of Captain Preston, Adams was to make another entry into his Diary, this time giving first the English translation and then the original:

> Every Act of Authority, of one Man over another for which there is not an absolute Necessity, is tyrannical.
>
> Le pene che oltre passano la necessità di conservare il deposito della Salute pubblica, sono ingiuste di lor natura.

Though the Italian text is not preserved today, we can at least know that Adams had an Italian edition, and that he might have even attempted to read it at one point or another.

In his entry of February-July 1780, for instance, he lists for July 7 as having paid to a certain Borzachini for two Italian Grammars and eleven lessons; on the following day, he paid a Mr. Molini for Baretti's Italian Dictionary, for Beccaria "Delliti e Pene" and for Buonmattei's *Grammatica*. Then, on July 27, he paid a Mr. Pechini "one Quarter" for his two sons--apparently for Italian lessons. And what may also be significant is that John Adams saw fit to bequeath Beccaria's book to one of his sons.

BEYOND CAPITAL PUNISHMENT

Although it is generally accepted that Beccaria was often quoted in connection with reforms of criminal laws, his influences encompassed a wider experience of human government. "Every Act of Authority", as quoted by John Adams in July of 1786, "of one Man over another for which there is not an absolute Necessity, is tyrannical." The paragraph from which Adams takes the quote comes at the end of Chapter II, and read as follows:

> Punishments meted out beyond the necessity to preserve the depositary of public health are, by their nature, unjust, as they are just when they make public security sacred and inviolable, thereby allowing the sovereign to preserve the greatest amount of liberty for his subjects.

Although *On Crimes and Punishments* may deal extensively with criminal law, Beccaria's message is wider in scope, as can be seen in the above short paragraph.

Beccaria hoped to have established a system of laws that might better serve all of humanity to achieve greater perfection and, therefore, greater utility and happiness.

He believed that this could be achieved through sound and just laws, that only through a responsible code of laws could men achieve maximum perfectibility as persons and as members of society.

Through the laws--only enough laws as necessary--could each man protect and be protected. Only through the laws could mankind save itself from returning to the state of primitive barbarism and bondage.

When in his, *The Ideological Origin of the American Revolution*, Bernard Bailyn states that in "pamphlet after pamphlet the American writers cited...Beccaria on the reform of criminal law," he is not altogether right because he restricts Beccaria's scope.

Beccaria was concerned with the overall betterment of human life. By restricting Beccaria to the reform of criminal law, Bailyn also limits the American writers by placing them in fixed categories of human experiences without considering that often the overlapping of these experiences may be more important.

Surely in Beccaria's case, when he makes of the laws the means to an end for mankind, he is not thinking of criminal laws only, though literally he does emphasize them. Thus, when John Adams quotes from Beccaria, "Every Act of Authority, of one Man over another for which there is not an absolute Necessity, is Tyrannical", he is surely not limiting himself to considerations of criminal laws; he is contemplating how mankind can govern itself through an Authority that must not be tyrannical at the same time.

"The Law Is King!" exclaims Thomas Paine in his pamphlet, *Common Sense*, in a paragraph reminiscent of Beccaria's fervor:

> But where, says some, is the King of America? I'll tell you. Friend, he reigns above, and doth not make havoc of mankind like the Royal Brute in Britain. Yet that we may not appear to be defective even in earthly honors, let a day be solemnly set apart for proclaiming the charter; let it be brought forth on the divine law, the Word of God; let a crown be placed thereon, by which the world may know, that so far we approve of monarchy, that in America *The Law Is King*. For as in absolute governments the King is law, so in free countries the law ought to be the king; and there ought to be no other. But lest any ill use should afterwards arise, let the crown at the conclusion of the ceremony, be demolished, and scattered among the people whose right it is.

Thomas Paine, a native of England, published the blistering pamphlet in January of 1776. It is strange that in it Paine does not quote from any of Beccaria's works. In fact, he does not even mention Beccaria, but quotes from Beccaria's contemporary and follower--Giacinto Dragonetti (1738-1818).

In 1766, Dragonetti published, anonymously, his *Delle virtú e dei premi* (On Virtues and Rewards) which complements Beccaria's book published two years earlier.

Dragonetti's book--like that of Beccaria, which received praise and fortune as a result of Voltaire 's demonstrated interest--also received praise from Diderot, who, in turn, imitated Dragonetti's work. But though Paine refers to Dragonetti, what he says sounds more like the thoughts if not the language of Beccaria:

> Should any body of men be hereafter delegated for this or some similar purpose, I offer them the following extracts from that wise observer of Governments, Dragonetti. "The science", says he, "of the Politician consists in fixing the true point of happiness and freedom. Those men would deserve the gratitude of ages, who should discover a mode of government that contained the greatest sum of individual happiness, with the least national expense. (*Common Sense*).

Practically the same ideas are expressed by Beccaria in his introduction:

> The laws were never dictated by a clear and cold examiner of human nature, who should concentrate in a particular point all the actions of a multitude of men, and should consider the laws from this point of view: maximum happiness divided among the greatest number of people. Happy are those few nations that passed good laws, without waiting for either slow motion of chance or of human vicissitudes to take place. In this manner, they avoided having to pass laws generated by existing evil situations for the well-being of the population. And that philosopher deserves the gratitude of mankind...for having planted the first seeds of useful truths.

In talking about the laws made by one generation of legislators and binding on the people of the future generations, Thomas Paine, in his *Rights of Man*, says that the "laws of every country must be analogous to some common principle." Then he expands on the argument:

> Those who have quitted the world, and those who are not yet arrived at it, are as remote from each other as the utmost stretch of mortal imagination can conceive. What possible obligation, then, can exist between them; what rule or principle can be laid down that of two nonentities, the one out of existence and the other not in, and who can never meet in this world, the one should control the other to the end of time?

Lacking the eloquence and intensity of Paine, Beccaria, the cool examiner of human nature, had already treated the same argument. Yet, though lacking the intensity of Paine, Beccaria becomes more poignant, calling "iniquitous" such laws as come down though oaths:

> The judges have not received the laws from our ancient forefathers, as we receive a domestic tradition or a testament requesting posterity the care to obey; they receive the laws from living society or from the sovereign who represents it as the legitimate depositary composed of everyone's will. They do not receive them conditioned by obligations of an ancient oath--such oaths would be void if not iniquitous if they were to be received, because they would bind men of different epochs without the possibility of agreement...

The necessity of good laws for a government, in order to guarantee the rights of the very people forming that government, was uppermost in the minds of Paine and of Adams, and of the rest of the enlightened founders of America's democracy. They believed, as Beccaria did, that good laws prevent criminal acts, for, "Crimes are acts of Tyranny of one or more on another or more." The laws also serve as a brake for those individuals bent on taking advantage of a people's temporary discontent in order to seize power and establish a despotic government worse than the one deposed, and utilizing the same men that helped in the seizure of the power. The citizens become the victims of themselves and serve as the means in maintaining another's tyranny.

In a country lacking good laws, the government leaves itself wide open to discontent and to its possible substitution through force. "Do you want to prevent crimes?" asks Beccaria, who considers the forceful overthrow of government a crime, then:

> Be sure that wise men be the companions of liberty. The evils that arise from knowledge are in inverse ratio to their diffusion whereas the benefits are in direct ratio. A daring impostor who is never an ordinary individual, is always adored by the masses and scorned by the enlightened... [But] when in a nation the enlightened individuals are profusely dispersed throughout the land, the slanderous ignorance will be silenced, and the authority which is disarmed by reason will tremble, leaving immobile the vigorous force of the laws; because there is no enlightened individual that does not

love the public, the clear, and the useful contracts of the common security, especially when comparing that little bit of useless liberty sacrificed by him with the maximum of all the liberties sacrificed by other men, who without laws, could become his conspirators.

BECCARIA AND JAMES WILSON

One of the great founding fathers at the level of James Madison, the Father of the Constitution, unsung to this day is Pennsylvania's James Wilson. Having signed the Declaration of Independence, he served as a delegate to the constitutional convention where he held sway over his colleagues "not by the charm of his eloquence, but by the force of his reasoning" (*Formation of the United States* p. 101). Among other things, he favored the following: equality of the executive, judiciary and of the legislative branches; term limitation for the executive; election of the executive and legislative branches by the people and not by the House or Senate; proportional representation; the abrogation of slave trade; the establishment of universities; and, independence in the name of the people--a union of men not of states--, to cite a few examples. With the convention a success, together with his other colleagues, Wilson signed the Constitution of the United States of America and saw it ratified.

Wilson's relation to Beccaria is well established in his own writings and observations, as edited by Robert Green McCoskey, *The Works of James Wilson*. Wilson makes extensive use of Beccaria's *On Crimes and Punishments*, often quoting long passages, with a passion reminiscent of John Adams, and almost equal to that of Beccaria himself.

On the question of forming a nation out of vast territorial expanses, Wilson quotes directly from Beccaria:

> An overgrown republick can be saved from despotism, only by subdividing it into a number of confederate republics. (p. 263)

In dealing with the issue of *honor*, Wilson makes an extremely interesting if not important observation in relation to despotism and liberty, striking a balance that may have served as the guiding force behind our formative documents. Of interest, too, is the difference in view between Montesquieu and Beccaria with regard to the definition of *honor*:

> It is the sentiment of some writers, highly distinguished too by their liberal and manly principles... [as with] the celebrated Montesquieu... that honour is peculiar to governments which are monarchial. "In extreme political liberty," says Marquis of Beccaria, "and in absolute despotism, all ideas of honour disappear, or are confounded with others. In the first case, reputation becomes useless from the despotism of the laws; and, in the second, the despotism of one man, annulling all civil existence, reduces the rest to a precarious temporary personality. Honour, then, is one of the fundamental principles of those monarchies, which are a limited despotism, and in these, like revolutions in despotick states, it is a momentary return to a state of nature and original equality. (pp. 594-95)

On the observation that the Americans were engaged in creating a government rather than reforming one, Wilson had understood that distinction from the very beginning, he having been raised in England and knowing too well the ways things were done there:

> To give you a history of the practice of criminal law would be a task, not difficult, because the materials are very copious... The English State Trials... are so disgraceful, not only to the nation, but to human nature, that, as they cannot be disbelieved, I wish them to be buried in oblivion. From oblivion, it is neither my duty nor inclination to rescue them. (p. 617)

The excitement if not the exultation of John Adams when citing Beccaria is repeated by Wilson in linguistic style and content:

> "How happy would mankind be," says the eloquent and benevolent Beccaria, "if laws were now to be first formed!" The United States enjoy this singular happiness. Their laws are now first formed. They are formed by the legitimate representatives of free citizens and free states. (p. 821)

TWO TYRANTS

It may be a strange coincidence that in talking about "daring impostors" both John Adams and Thomas Paine should have used two figures from Italian history, men who, on taking advantage of the political crisis of the moment, and by duping the crowd, were able to overthrow the governments and assume power for themselves. But, the very mob that made possible the seizure, on feeling a more despotic form of government from the same individuals, who had, among other things, promised liberty and given otherwise, on discovering the true nature of the impostors, reacted with as much swiftness in murdering the despots as they did in destroying the legal but otherwise ineffective prior government.

In his *Common Sense*, Paine urges the colonists to proclaim a Charter with which to establish the independence of the colonies from England:

> A government of our own is our natural right: and when a man seriously reflects on the precariousness of human affairs, he will become convinced, that it is infinitely wiser and safer, to form a constitution of our own in a cool deliberate manner, while we have it in our power, than to trust such an interesting event to time and chance. If we omit it now, some Massanello may hereafter arise, who, laying hold of popular disquietudes, may collect

> together the desperate and the discontented, and by assuming to themselves the powers of government, finally sweep away the liberties of the Continent like a deluge.

Thomas Aniello (1620-1647), otherwise known by his Neapolitan nickname of Masaniello, was the leader of the popular successful revolt of 1647 which pitted the Neapolitans against the tyrannical government of the Spaniards. Immediately after the revolt, the people made him their captain. But soon, Masaniello took advantage of his power and began to overstep his authority. When he reverted to cruelty in order to achieve his goals, those same people, who had made him their captain, quickly killed him in the same year he had gotten into power.

John Adams, writing his Diary in the summer of 1798, reflected on another character from Italy, the Roman, Cola Di Rienzo (1314-1354), a forerunner of the late Duce.

Cola envisioned a second Roman Empire with Rome at its center. In attempting to fulfill his dreams, he organized the various free communes of Italy in opposition to the nobility and to the church, whose exiled Pope was living in Avignon. Having been defeated by the latter, Cola was exiled to Prague. Upon his release, he returned to Rome as a free man. Once again, he organized the people and succeeded in establishing a new government for the city of Rome. At first, the people fought for him and assured him the throne. But soon, he became infatuated with his power and began to abuse the very people that had empowered him. The people revolted and amassed beneath his palace. Shrewd as he was unpredictable, Cola dressed in disguise secretly made his way into the heart of the mob, shouting with them, "Down with Cola; kill Cola." Then, the story goes, something went wrong with the disguise and he was recognized. Thereupon and without hesitation, the crowd turned on him and killed him right on the spot.

Reflecting on Cola, John Adams is reminiscent of Beccaria's observations in attempting to answer why these incidents take place. In his opinion, such incidents are generated by defective and outdated laws, which in turn give way to despotism.

It must be accepted that in the minds of the founders of America's government, the concern of wanting to avert such despotism must have been of tantamount importance. It cannot be a pure coincidence that in the many years over which America's democracy has been in force, it has not had any such usurpations. The reason must be due to safeguards incorporated in the documents that made America's democracy possible, documents that have allowed us to guard against a Masaniello or a Cola or even a more redoubtable Robespierre.

It is interesting to note Adams's observations over Petrarch, the famous Italian poet, and Cola, as he writes in his Diary on July 31, 1796:

> Reading the second Volume of Petrarch's Life. This singular character had very wild Notions of the Right of the City of Rome to a Republican Government and the Empire of the World. It is strange that his Infatuation for [Cola di] Rienzi did not expose him to more Resentment and greater Danger. In the Absence of the Pope at Avignon, and the People having no

regular Check upon the Nobles, these fell into their usual Dissentions, and oppressed the People till they were ripe to be duped by any single Enthusiast, bold Adventurer, ambitious Usurper, or hypocritical Villain who should, with sufficient Imprudence, promise them justice, (Humanity), Clemency, and Liberty.

A FEDERATION OF STATES

Confronted with a vast land area over which to govern, the early Americans like Adams, Washington, and Jefferson, surely must have thought about the problem of governing such an extensive territory without having to resort to despotism. Beccaria had considered the question, saying that "a too vast republic cannot save itself from despotism unless it subdivides itself into so many little federal republics."

Yet, when the time came to ratify the Constitution, which was to govern the federated states, the question of "We, the States" or "We, the People" was highly contested. Charles Pinkney, Elbridge Gerry and others opted for the former; James Madison, James Wilson and others opted for the latter. In the end, "We, the People" won out, thus forcefully maintaining the recurrent spirit of emphasizing the single individual rather than an entity to assume the responsibility of government.

Regardless of how many smaller republics a nation may divide itself into, according to Beccaria, it always has to be a "union of people" all counted as individual citizens. When, on the other hand, a society or a nation is based on units such as states or families, then we have a union of families or of states and not a union of people. It follows that in Beccaria's mind, there would not exist categories of people, no special privileges for the clergy or categories of the nobility, no "whites" or "blacks", no homosexuals or feminists. These, and others not mentioned, would compose the "union of people" with equal rights under the supreme law of "We, the People". His observations, therefore, make sense:

> If there are one hundred thousand men, or rather twenty thousand families each consisting of five members including the head who represents the family, and the association of the society is made of families, then there would be twenty thousand men and eighty thousand slaves. But if the association is composed of men, there would be one hundred thousand citizens and no slaves. In the first case there would be a republic together with twenty thousand little monarchies; in the second instance, the republican spirit will breathe not only in the public squares and in the nation's assemblies, but in each home as well where the greater part of men's happiness and misery is to be found.

The extent to which Beccaria's observation served to cause the Founding Fathers to opt for "We, the People" over "We, the States" may never be completely known. But that the Constitution was supposed to be the supreme law of the land has certainly come to fruition. It is this kind of law, a law that aims at the single individual rather than at units, that Beccaria was principally concerned with, it being the means to regulate the activities of men and to assure them their happiness on earth.

To continue to insist that Beccaria was influential only with the reforms of criminal law does injustice to him as a man and as a philosopher.

In the case of Europe, he had tremendous impact because there was dire need to reform the criminal laws. But in America the need was to secure laws that would guarantee a form of government of the people, by the people, and for the people; and Beccaria's book, if it was at all influential, was so in this respect: not having had the right to reform laws, our forefathers created them, and Beccaria was influential in shaping the basic code of American laws.

> When the republic is made up of men, the family does not become subordinate to command, but becomes subordinate to contract instead; and the children, when they are of age when they are free from dependence on nature--which consists of that weakness and need of education and of self-protection--then they become free members of the city, and become subjects of their own free will to the head of the family in partaking of the advantages as do the free men of a great society. In the first case, the children--which form the greater part and the most useful to the nation--are at the discretion of the father; in the second case, there exists but one tie of command, which is that sacred and inviolable tie of administering reciprocally the necessary succor, and that of gratitude for the received benefits, which gratitude is not so much destroyed by the malice of the human heart as by a misunderstood subjection by the laws.

It might be added at this point that in the society of Beccaria, there are no nobles by birthright, for the system of the nobility automatically and historically forms family units and breathes a caste system that benefits the few at the expense of the many.

In her book, *Jefferson, the Road to Glory 1743-1776*, Marie Kimball insists on the traditional concept of Beccaria's role as the one responsible for the reform of criminal laws. She proves her point through Jefferson, who without doubt admired Beccaria's book. "Revision of the laws concerning crimes and punishments lay in Jefferson's particular sphere as a revisor", says Kimball; then she states that Jefferson had "no less than 25 extracts from Beccaria", and that Jefferson "absorbed Beccaria's ideas, along with those of many other writers, by the time he started to prepare his 'Bill for proportioning crimes and punishments in cases heretofore capital."

While these observations are true, to limit oneself to parroting the same remarks is to limit the thrust of Beccaria's book, especially in connection with individuals of the calibre of Jefferson, the man and the driving force behind the creation--and not the formation or revision--of the body of laws that were to be accepted as "the King".

Were the scope of Beccaria to be limited to crime and punishment, as purported by the title, the book should contain an abundance of words such as *crime* and *punishment*. The fact is that Beccaria frequently, if not compulsorily used such words as *law, liberty, rights, justice, republic, human being, poor wretch, tyranny, happiness*--the conclusion being that where there are good laws the people enjoy various degrees of happiness; whereas, where there are bad laws, the people endure various degrees of unhappiness. The former liberates; the latter subjugates--that is the basic message in Beccaria's book.

Vittorio Alfieri, a contemporary of Beccaria, may have given the best definition of tyranny:

> *Any government whatever in which those having the responsibility for the execution of the laws become tyrants when they make or destroy them, break them, interpret them, impede them or even only delude them with the security of impunity.*

A tyrant utilizes the laws as he sees fit and the laws become his tool. Citizens must guard against elected or appointed individuals who make laws for their personal gains. Consider the perks, the special privileges, the preferential treatments, the compensations, the retirements, and one should quickly see the use that elected and appointed officials make of their offices. Measuring this abuse could be done through an analysis of the individual net worth at the beginning and at the end of each term in office. When the difference is exorbitant, then it becomes obvious that that individual acted like a tyrant and used the present laws or designed new laws for personal benefits and not for the benefit of the people. It is precisely this type of tyranny that men such as Jefferson, Madison, Adams, Washington and others fought to avoid.

In the Declaration of Independence, the intention is expressed much as Beccaria might have wished:

> When in the Course of human events, it becomes necessary for one people to dissolve the

> political bands which have connected them with another, and to assume among the powers of the earth, the separate and equal station to which the Laws of Nature and of Nature's God entitle them, a decent respect to the opinions of mankind requires that they should declare the causes which impel them to the separation. We hold these truths...

After this very eloquent and sustained introduction, wherein equality of mankind is defined within the limits of the laws, the Representatives of the future United States of America assembled in General Congress on July 4, 1776 to spell out their past history in connection with the tyranny of the English King, as follows:

> The History of the present King of Great Britain is a History of repeated injuries and Usurpations, all having in direct Object the Establishment of an absolute Tyranny over these States. To prove this, let the Facts be submitted to a candid World.

What follows is the enumeration of 27 Facts that more than prove their claims. The first four, however seem the most significant:

> He has refused his Assent to Laws, the most wholesome and necessary for the Public Good.
>
> He has forbidden his Governors to pass Laws of immediate and pressing Importance, unless suspended in their Operation till his Assent should be obtained; and when so sus-

> pended, he has utterly neglected to attend them.
>
> He has refused to pass other Laws for the Accommodation of large Districts of People, unless those People could relinquish the Right of Representation in the Legislature, a Right inestimable to them and formidable to Tyrants only.
>
> He has called together Legislative Bodies at Places unusual, uncomfortable, and distant from the Depository of their public Records, for the sole Purpose of fatiguing them into Compliance with his Measures.

The culprit has a name: the King, responsible for a lack of good laws and for passing too many bad laws. He was the tyrant who affected the laws on his behalf. He, after all, existed for himself and the people existed for him. "He had refused his Assent to Laws, the most wholesome and necessary for the Public Good." The American Founding Fathers were no fools. Tyrants came then--as they come now--in different garb. Underneath, however, they are still tyrants.

In view of those abuses, it is no wonder that the 57 men--20 of whom lawyers--should conclude to support the Declaration of Independence by pledging to each other *their lives, their fortunes, and their sacred honor*; for, in the conditions under which they were living, their lives, their fortunes, and their honor had little if any meaning.

One of the signers was the 33 year-old lawyer-farmer from Virginia--Thomas Jefferson; the other was the 40 year-old lawyer from Massachusetts--John Adams. These two men are singled out for the role they played in stating the conditions under which they were living in the colonies. What was additionally needed was another document to incorporate safeguards against the very things they were suffering.

With the Constitution of 1787, the ideals of the Declaration of Independence having been transcribed therein, and with it the procedures through which to form and run the new government were established. Remarkable is the clarity of the language which aims at the essence of things rather than on their details--and this is perhaps why the document is still guiding a nation that has seen a geometric growth in territory and in population since the memorable year of 1787.

In his chapter on crime prevention, Beccaria speaks of laws in general. His observations, however, are applicable across the board; and the implications, for sure, reach beyond the field of criminal laws:

> Do you want to prevent crime? Then be sure that the laws are clear and simple, and that the whole strength of the nation be considered in order to defend them and that no part of that strength be employed to destroy them. Make sure that the laws favor less the various classes of men and more and more the individual men themselves.

There are not, nor should there be classes of men, unless we mistake or misunderstand the meaning and implications of "We, the People". How much clearer can this message be? What words of other laws can be as clear as "We, the People"? If there is no other law as supreme, why should its implementation not yet be completed?

The language of Beccaria and that of his American counterparts is as clear as it is concise in establishing that whatever is done is to be done for the people, and that the strength of the nation be utilized to defend rather than to destroy the laws, remembering that good laws are those reflecting the needs of the entire population.

BECCARIA AND THE FIRST AMENDMENT

The rights of the people are further strengthened in the first ten amendments to the Constitution known as the Bill of Rights.

In his book, *A History of Italian Literature*, Ernest Hatch Wilkins, one of the first American scholars to point out the importance of Beccaria to early American thought, speaks about Beccaria's book:

> The treatise was immediately and very widely influential. It was translated into a score of languages, and led to the revisions of several penal codes. The first English translation appeared in 1767; a reprint of that translation issued in New York in 1773 is, with a single unimportant exception, the first translation on an Italian work to be published in this country. The influence of Beccaria's thought is manifest in the American Bill of Rights.

ESTABLISHMENT OF RELIGION:

The First Amendment of the Bill of Rights is perhaps the most far-reaching in that it prohibits Congress from passing laws that might respect the "establishment of religion, or prohibiting the free exercise thereof."

What turns out to be separation of church and state, and, in any event, the freedom of the people to practice whatever civilized form of religion they wish--both on an individual or collective level, is an extension of Beccaria's desire as expressed in the chapter on a "particular kind of crime".

Without mentioning the crimes committed under the name of religion, Beccaria nevertheless makes us understand what the early Americans understood all too well to put into practice: that while all other nations have had religious strife, with the exception of local incidents as the hanging of Mary Dyer in the Boston Commons, or the witch-hunting in Salem, Massachusetts, the United States of America has not undergone the frightening crimes related to religious activities. Without a doubt, this is due to the farsightedness of those who wrote the First Amendment.

Modern Americans who consider the perfunctory recital of empty prayer words in public schools may well consider Beccaria's worries:

> Reasonable men will see that the place, the century, and the subject matter do not permit me to examine the nature of such crimes. It would take me too long and far wide from my subject matter in order to prove how...opinions which differ from each other only by some very subtle and obscure variances, altogether beyond human capability to understand, how they can still upset the public welfare when one opinion is not authorized in preference over the others.

Yet, no where does Beccaria make any statement against the practice of religion either by individuals or groups. On the other hand, he upholds the right of freedom of religion, which freedom ceases to exist as soon as, by act of law, any part of any religion becomes the official representative of any arm of government.

Prayer in school, of whatever form or non-form, can only be accomplished through the enactment and execution of some sort of law. Attempts on implementing school prayers have failed. That failure is not a reflection of a Godless society or of insensitive lawgivers. Certainly Americans actively follow many religions. As certain, the Founding Fathers, without exception, were very religious. But they saw the harm done to individuals and societies as a result of religious misapplication. They sought to avoid those situations for their own and future generations, and thanks to them, they succeed for own good. Therefore, there cannot be laws which are clear but not executable, nor unclear laws that are executable. Legislating on religion only creates paradox. Legislating on the clergy presents similar difficulties.

"The principle of Beccaria is sound", says Jefferson in contemplating the laws that gave the clergy special privileges. Yet there is no need to have any type of pardons specified by either the legislature or by the executive, for, "when laws are made as mild as they should be...pardons are absurd. The principle of Beccaria is sound. Let the legislators be merciful, but the executors of the law inexorable."

The clergy have to be as responsible to the laws as are other citizens; and, as no one can receive special privileges through legislation, religion--no matter how neutral (neutrality would nullify religion)--must not be officially recognized by any part of a constituted government.

The belief that a little bit of religion cannot do harm especially among the young, and in the morning before classes, is a view held by many well-intentioned people. They do not realize, however, that habit, as observed by Beccaria, is often the worst of tyrants. The fact is that, in twentieth century America, prayer continues to be an issue with its potential for strife ever present.

We should reiterate Beccaria's observation on what happens when one opinion is authorized over another; how, as a result, this preference can upset the public welfare, and even bring about revolts and wars. In any event, receptivity of religious forms or practices cannot be enforced except when done by despotic means.

FREEDOM OF SPEECH:

One's opinion has to be respected; as important, its expression must be allowed, especially in politics. In Beccaria's words, "opinion, which is the best, or perhaps, the only cement of society, may curb the authority of the powerful."

Freedom of speech allows us to state our opinions; freedom of the press allows us the means to transmit them if we wish, and there cannot be legislation to prevent it from taking place. In addition, no public official should be allowed to force receptivity of their opinions onto the private citizens. To the contrary, the people must insure that their public officials be receptive of their opinions and feelings, and that they should never allow their officials to avoid, thwart, limit, or eliminate that receptivity; otherwise, the citizens would not be able to hold their officials accountable. If opinion, then, is the "cement of society", society must see to it that proper binding take place at every level of society. But how?

When laws are written in a way that they cannot be easily interpreted, it causes the citizens to seek the services of lawyers. When this happens, the laws, "instead of being public and general, are thus rendered private and particular." But through well written laws, power is "vested in the whole, and not in any part of the society." And there is no better way to achieve it than through freedom of speech or of the press. As an adjunct, freedom of the press or "the use of printing, which alone makes the public, and not a few individuals, the guardians and defenders of the laws"--by allowing the people to exchange their opinions without impunity--guarantees healthy exchanges, enlightenment, regeneration, and growth both of individuals and their societies.

In Beccaria and in the First Amendment, freedom of the press emphasizes the free and unincumbered transmission of opinion through "the use of printing" aimed at dissipating "the gloomy spirit of cabal and of intrigue, and, not the re-creation or repetition of past cabal and intrigue. The question for the people to ask is if the press--the media--has advanced freedom of speech or set it back; whether the press is the vehicle through which people can enlighten themselves or once again the vehicle for "secret treasons", "public massacres", or of "ministers of the gospel of Christ, bathing their hands in blood, in the name of the God of all mercy."

Freedom of speech or of the press, in the First Amendment and as clarified by Beccaria, is the means to an end for the people, and not for the few who administer the press, or of those in official positions. The latter should use the press only to inform the people of their official enactments and not to use it for personal gains be it of power or of wealth.

Precisely because opinions have the same basis as religious beliefs, Congress shall make no law to establish state religions or abridge the freedom of speech or of the press. The abridgement of either or of both has to be left to customs, to common sense, to public gatherings and assemblies, or whatever, in order to achieve a degree of balance derived from popular consensus and not from enacted laws or regulations.

THE REFORMER

It seems fair to say that Beccaria's role on the European scene was that of a reformer. The fact that so many codes were changed either directly or indirectly as a result of his book surely made him the reformer. France changed its constitutional provision for capital punishment; other monarchies followed suit. In Italy, capital punishment was abolished. These things were possible because there were bad laws in need of reform or revision.

In America, however, where the early Americans depended on someone else's laws, there were no laws as such to reform or to revise. Their choice was of obeying or not obeying. On discovering that the English King was practicing his tyranny on them through English-made laws, they rebelled and did something about it.

"He has refused his Assent to laws, the most wholesome and necessary for the Public Good" was the first fact they enumerated. Their goal, therefore, was not to reform--a right they did not have--but to reject in order to create, all the while risking losing their lives, let alone their fortunes and honor. Fate wanted that they should succeed in achieving their independence, and thereby set the stage in initiating the last phase of a historical cycle with the ratification of the Constitution.

Having been part of that creation, Beccaria was also present in the north American continent by way of English common laws introduced here almost a century later mainly through the works of William Blackstone.

His *Commentaries on the Laws of England* published in London in 1769, together with later editions, was considered a cornerstone for understanding English present and future common laws. In the next century, it was of immense importance to America.

> Sir William Blackstone's *Commentaries* is the most important legal treatise ever written in the English language. It was the dominant law book in England and in America in the century after its publication and played a unique role in the development of the fledgling American legal system. (p. III)

There is no question as to Blackstone's role in reforming the laws of England and those of America. Practically every author, writing books on this subject, has to deal with Blackstone, but many American authors writing books on Blackstone continuously fail to deal with Beccaria. The fact is, however, that every time Blackstone makes a visit to America, in whatever form, Beccaria inescapably re-visits the country whose government he had helped to shape. It is not strange, therefore, to see Beccaria come in again through the work of others. And each time he comes back, he returns as the reformer, hardly quoted even if at times admired, but hardly mentioned in connection with his role as a spiritual founding father as has been shown in the previous pages.

In his *Crime and the Courts in England* published in 1986, J. M. Beattie makes several observations on the role that Beccaria played in England:

> ...the capacity of the law and the administrative system to deal with crime and social disorder became...a subject of wider concern and discussion than had been apparent earlier. The discussion was undoubtedly encouraged by the publication in 1767 of an English translation of Beccaria's tract *Of Crimes and Punishments*, in which the basis of the established system, in England as elsewhere, was called into question. But the debate was carried forward in print and in parliament by Blackstone, Eden and others. (pp. 222-23)

On the more specific question of crime and punishment, Beattie makes other interesting observations on Beccaria's influence in England and on Europe:

> Beccaria's tract made a considerable impression and produced a violent debate in Europe... [He] clearly had some immediate influence in England. Blackstone's ideas of punishment, for example, show evidence of it. In the 4th volume of his *Commentaries*...which appeared two years after Beccaria's English translation, he addressed himself to general questions of punishment...(pp. 555-56). In 1771 William Eden...published his *Principles of Penal Law*...clearly much influenced by Beccaria... (p.558). A program advocated in the writings of Beccaria and Howard was quickly adopted after 1776, on paper at least, and it seems likely that these men had been avidly read because they justified courses of action that a significant number of men in positions of authority in the

localities as well as in parliament had come to believe in. (pp. 628-29)

EDITIONS OF *On Crimes And Punishments*

The first edition of *Dei delitti e delle pene* appeared in Livorno, Italy, in July 1764, printed and published by a certain Coltellini of Livorno. At the time of publication, Beccaria was twenty-six years old.

A second edition, revised and corrected, appeared during the same year in Monaco. This edition had 112 pages--eight more than the first edition.

The third edition appeared the following year in Lausanne. This edition contained 229 pages. The additional pages were due to the various answers Beccaria wrote in response to criticism and to charges that were published against his book and against him as a person. This edition also included the first additions on the part of the author to the basic text. The book, however, found its way into the listing of the Roman *Index* through the efforts of the preacher Fachinei, who harshly criticized Beccaria.

In 1766 there appeared two editions in Harlem; in 1767, another in Buglion, France. Subsequently there appeared in Dublin another with an English translation and a commentary attributed to M. de Voltaire; this edition was published in Dublin but printed by J. Exshaw. A similar edition appeared in London the same year. Another appeared in London in 1769 and one in 1770 together with another in Glasgow.

In America, the first edition in translation supposedly appeared in print in 1773, as it was advertised as "in press" by the Rivington, New York, Gazetteer on 28 October 1773. A copy of this edition has not yet been found. The earliest edition of which there are still some copies, appeared in Philadelphia in 1776, and includes the commentary attributed to Voltaire. In 1777, another edition appeared in Charlestown, South Carolina; it was printed and sold by David Bruce, at his shop on Church Street. The title page indicates that the commentary is attributed to Voltaire; it does not show Beccaria as the author of the book, however. In 1778, another edition appeared in Philadelphia, printed and sold by R. Bell, next door to St. Paul's Church, on Third Street. Ten years later, another edition appeared in South Carolina. Meanwhile, other editions had appeared in Dublin, London, Glasgow, etc. Several editions appeared in Edinburgh alone. During this time, the book appeared in translation in practically every cultural center of Europe and America.

It may be added as an item of curiosity that the first of Voltaire's works published in colonial America was his *The Man Worth Forty Crowns*, appearing in Philadelphia in 1778. In the same year, his *Miscellanies* appeared, and in 1796 came out his *Philosophical Dictionary*. Rousseau's *Confessions*, on the other hand, was first published in America in 1796. *The Spirit of the Law* of Montesquieu--Beccaria's idol in more ways than one--was first published in America in 1802. It might also be added that, according to *The National Union Catalog Pre-1956 Imprints*, William Young, in his "A new edition corrected", erroneously lists the edition as having been published in 1763, and Beccaria born in 1735.

In the twentieth century, Beccaria's book continues to be translated. In 1963, H. Paolucci made a translation which was published by Bobbs-Merrill. The following year, K. Foster and J. Grigson translated it in England, publishing it under the title of *The Column of Infamy*, a work written by Beccaria's grandson, Alessandro Manzoni, author of *I Promessi Sposi*.

Beccaria's works have recently been published by Sansoni of Florence. The two volumes edited by Sergio Romagnoli contain all of Beccaria's works, including his poetry and essay on Style, as well as Romagnoli's ample introduction and bibliographical notes. Nowhere in the two volumes does Romagnoli mention either Adams or Jefferson, or the editions that appeared in the United States around the time of the Revolution.

In 1879 it was translated and published in Russian; in 1982 and in 1989, two editions appeared in the German language.

In 1984, Gianni Francioni edited a new edition published in Milano by Mediobanca; another edition edited by Rosalba Canetta and also published by Mediobanca appeared in 1987. David Young made a new translation from the Italian and was published by Hackett in Indianapolis in 1986.

The reason for so many editions might be due to one fact--the issues raised by Beccaria have not been resolved; and many scholars with many humanitarian reformers may feel that in Beccaria we may still find the inspiration if not the solutions to some of our grave problems such as *capital punishment, secret accusations, gun control, public prayer, crime prevention, law reforms, abortion*, and others.

BECCARIA LIFE AND TIME

The life of Beccaria, a young eighteenth century nobleman, was hardly predictable as having influence on the revolutionary epoch then germinating. Marquis Cesare Bonesana di Beccaria was born of an aristocratic family on March 15, 1738 in Milan, Italy, where he also died in 1794. As a child, he was educated by the Jesuits of Parma. In 1758, he received his law degree from the University of Pavia, dissatisfied, however, with the type of education he had received. Against his father's wishes, Beccaria married a certain Teresa Blasco in 1761, breaking his relations with his father, and quickly finding himself in poverty.

At the age of twenty-two, he began to read the authors of the Enlightenment, especially Montesquieu, whose *Lettres Persanes* made possible his intellectual conversion. This conversion must have been reinforced through his participation in the challenging discussions held by a group of friends belonging to the academy of *Pugni*. These, no doubt, inspired and most likely also collaborated with him.

During this time, there were many such groups in Italy, often going under the names of academies. Among the more important ones, the *Academia dei Pugni* was founded by Pietro Verri in 1760. Its members, proposing to deal with various cultural aspects of the period as promulgators and as educators of the new culture, published their thoughts in their literary magazine entitled *Caffè*, appearing in Brescia every ten days. Beccaria became one of their more important members. The others were the Verri brothers, and Frisi, Bitti, Lambertenghi, Visconti, Longo, and others. With the exception of Beccaria, above all, and of the Verri Brothers, none of the original members achieved any fame.

The other two academies were the *Granelleschi*, which was founded in Venice by the Gozzi brothers, and that of the *Trasformati* of which the poet Parini was a member. The three vied to do several things and were often at odds with one another. That of the *Pugni*, for instance, wished to introduce foreign elements into a stifled Italian culture; that of the *Granelleschi* wished to retain the purity of the Italian culture and fought against the introduction of foreign elements; and that of the *Trasformati* maintained a middle-of-the road policy. Among the better known men of this time were: Parini, who published his very famous didactic-satirical poem, *Il Giorno* (The Day), begun in 1760; Alfieri, who wrote Shakespearean tragedies and two formidable political essays, *Della Tirannide* (On Tyranny) in 1777, and *Del Principe e delle lettere* (The Prince and Men of Letters) in 1786; and Giuseppe Baretti with his magazine *Frusta letteraria* (Literary Whip), founded in 1763, through which he attempted to rejuvenate Italian culture.

Beccaria participated in this challenging period of transition that later was to bring forth authors of the caliber of Ugo Foscolo, Giacomo Leopardi, and Alessandro Manzoni. Although Beccaria never achieved the literary fame or status of his colleagues in Italy, he gained a greater international prominence with his treatise.

It is doubtful that Beccaria would have written his book had it not been for the suggestion given him by his friends of the academy. In a sense, they assigned him the topic on the status of criminal law as it was practiced in Europe. Luckily, he accepted.

Immediately upon its publication, the book received wide acclaim and the usual severe criticism. With the translation by Morellet, the book appeared in France, where it received a cool reception, as witnessed by the indifferent appraisal by D'Alembert, the great French philosopher; however, upon reading the second edition, he suddenly became an admirer of the work, together with Diderot and Voltaire, both of whom wrote commentaries on Beccaria's treatise. It also received praise and endorsement from many other great men, including, Holbach, Helvetius, Buffon, Thomas, Hume, and even Hegel.

It is generally agreed that the tremendous success must have been due to the manner in which Beccaria brought into focus the subject of the deplorable state of crime and punishment in relation to criminal laws and procedures. His effect was so immediate that Catherine II of Russia invited Beccaria to Petersburg along with Voltaire. The Italian officials, under rule of Austria, decided to create the Beccaria Chair in Milan, thus compelling Beccaria to remain in Italy. While holding this Chair, as professor of economics, in his lectures he anticipated the economic theories of Adam Smith and the theories of Thomas Malthus on population and subsistence.

He left Italy, however, to visit Paris--a trip he could not refuse due to the clamorous and persistent invitation from the residents of the universally accepted cultural capital of the world. He made the journey to

Paris, together with his friend Pietro Verri. But the fanfare and the tremendous attention directed toward him was too much for him. Because of his inability to capitalize on his fame, Beccaria decided to return to Italy, leaving his friend Verri to continue with the celebration. Rumor had it that Beccaria was anxious to return to Italy so that he could be with his newly married wife, a young woman by the name of Anna from the family of Count Barnaba of Barbo.

On April 29, 1771, Beccaria was elected a member of the Supreme Council of the economy. He was active more or less in this capacity until 1791 when he was made a member of the official group whose goal was to reform the civil and criminal judicial system of Italy. He died November 28, 1794.

Cesare Beccaria lived during the time of the Enlightenment, the American Revolution, and later the abortive French Revolution. Like most intellectuals of the time, he came under the sway of the Cartesian philosophy which upheld the supremacy of the nation over the sensitive individual. Yet, though he was to receive the main stimulus for his work from the *Lettres Persanes* of Montesquieu, and from the *Contract Social* of Rousseau, Beccaria asserted that society is composed of individuals willing to give up a small part of their liberty--the least possible part--in order to achieve a common utility structured for all individuals in a given society. He describes it in this way:

> Laws are the conditions with which independent and isolated men united into society, being tired of having lived in a continuous state of war and of having enjoyed a liberty made useless by the uncertainty of not being able to

> conserve it. They sacrificed part of their liberty in order to enjoy what was left of it in security and tranquility. The sum total of these portions of liberty sacrificed to the welfare of each man, form the sovereignty of a nation whose ruler is the legitimate depository and administrator...
>
> Necessity, therefore, compelled men to give up a portion of individual liberty; it is certain, therefore, that each man does not want to place in the public depository but the least portion possible, just enough to compel others to defend him.

What may be unusual is the fact that Beccaria amplified on an observation made by Rousseau. But what may turn out to be more unusual is the possibility that Beccaria may have been affected by the Vichian philosophy of Giambattista Vico rather than by that of the enlightened Encyclopedists whose source, without a doubt, was Cartesian.

The Encyclopedists, for example, would never say, in attempting to solve human problems, "Let us look into our hearts" for answers. They turned to the rational mind instead because for them, the mind was the depository and source of all human experience. Beccaria, on the other hand, said that whatever is based on the sentiment of man is apt to be good.

> From political morality we cannot hope for any lasting advantages unless it is founded on indelible sentiments of man. Whatever law that should deviate from these sentiments will always encounter with a contrary resistance which in the end will always win out, just as a

small force evenly distributed will eventually win over any violent motion exerted to a mass.

Beccaria refers to the *sentiments of man*, a phrase that became highly evocative in his American counterparts, but practically absent from the vocabulary of the men of the Enlightenment, meant only from the point of view that sentiment is places in opposition to the pure mind or thought process. The first to contradict this principle may have been Vico in his *New Science* of 1725, wherein he affirms that *Nihil est intellectu quin prius fuerit in sensu* (Nothing is in the intellect which was not first in the senses).

Vico further took a different position on the role of intellect, reflection and philosophic logic. He placed fantasy against intellect, intuition against reflection, and poetic logic against philosophical logic. In other words, Vico reasserts man's sentiments as being at the base of all his present and future experiences. How man *feels* and what he *feels*, therefore, may disclose a superior sense of justice than might be gotten from a purely intellectualized process.

From this may follow that in Beccaria the idea or sense of justice is brought down to a human level--better still, justice is brought down to the *sensitive* level through which man is humanized. The principles, then, through which man is to be punished, should he transgress, are to be found in our hearts.

"Let us consult the human heart", Beccaria says, for, "in it, we will find the fundamental principles of the sovereign's true rights to punish crimes."

Beccaria is confident of man's sensibility. He places more faith on the role of man's heart solving the more crucial problems of man's relations to other men than on man's intellect, which too often leads him astray. But Beccaria does not say that the opposite is not also true. In this respect, he goes counter to that whole movement that finally culminated in the French Revolution.

The roots of Beccaria's philosophy must reside in Vico's historiography wherein Vico speaks of the courses and re-courses of history, dividing the cycle of history as revolving around three basic stages that keep on repeating themselves more or less consistently--the three stages being that of the Gods or the supernatural, that of the Heroes of the type of Achilles, and that of Man. The latter state would deal with those relationships which, in their application, limit the roles of the supernatural and of the heroic, and emphasize the role of men in their social interaction with the overall goal of achieving maximum happiness for the largest number of people.

To what extent does Beccaria base himself on Vico? The question is appropriate especially when Beccaria approaches his subject matter in much the same manner as Vico. "Moral and political principles which regulate mankind come from three sources: revelation, natural law, and man-made conventions", says Beccaria, who then goes on to discuss the various relationships among the three. (Vico had spoken of the three stages: that of the supernatural, that of the heroes, and that of Man).

Gianbattista Vico was very little known and accepted during his lifetime; his writings were even less understood. As a result, he came to be known as the obscure philosopher who did nothing more than amass thousands of details indiscriminately put down in forms incomprehensible to his contemporaries. The problem was not Vico's, however; but it must have centered around the manner in which he proceeded with his exposition. He moved in single units which he called *degnità*--basic units of truth that governed the universe with all that is in it. These basic units, also known as axioms, may be the ones that Beccaria refers to when contemplating the role of legislation through which mankind is to secure its happiness.

> ...that philosopher deserves the gratitude of mankind for having had the courage (from the detested and obscure study) of planting among the people the first seeds--for so long unharvested--of the useful truths.

That Vico may be that philosopher has not been suggested; yet, it is difficult to discard that possibility. Likewise, it is difficult to reject altogether the possibility that Thomas Paine may also have had some knowledge of Vico's historiography, especially when, in his *Rights of Man*, he states a Vichian observation: "First was a Government of Priestcraft, the second of Conquerors, and the third of Reason."

If with "that philosopher" Beccaria refers to Vico, then we can say that those "first seeds...of useful truths" did not go unharvested for too long a time, considering that the book *On Crimes and Punishments* may possibly be the first fruit to mature and to be harvested.* It can also be added without fear that the useful truths uncovered in Beccaria's book have been incorporated in practically all of the constitutions of the countries of Europe. The same truths which matured in the mind of Beccaria and transcribed in that little book also reached the new continent, penetrating into those lofty spirits who said:

> We hold these Truths to be self-evident, that all Men are created equal, that they are endowed by their Creator with certain unalienable Rights, that among these are Life, Liberty, and the Pursuit of Happiness--That to secure these Rights, Governments are instituted among Men, deriving their just Powers from the Consent of the Governed, that whenever any Form of Government becomes destructive of these Ends, it is the right of the People to alter or to abolish it, and to a institute new government, laying its Foundation on such Principles, and organizing its Powers in such Form, as to them shall seem likely to effect their Safety and happiness.

Thus the possibility that the above document may have initiated the third phase or stage of Vico's historiography wherein Man comes into being.

This axiom proves that there exists divine Providence, and that there is a divine legislative mind which has made possible for men to live in a human society through civil order, who otherwise would live as beasts in the wilderness, because every man is guided by the passion to seek out his own interests first.

---

*Here is an example expressed in *Degnità VII*: Legislation considers man what he is, in order to assign him those tasks that are amenable to his capabilities, for the good of the society; in the manner in which brutality, avarice, and ambition can bring humanity to its perdition, the soldier, the merchant, and the court, on the other hand, can bring strength, opulence, and knowledge to the republic. The three vices would certainly destroy mankind and preclude man from achieving the desired civil happiness.

John Adams.

Frontespiece of Adam's copy with code of arms

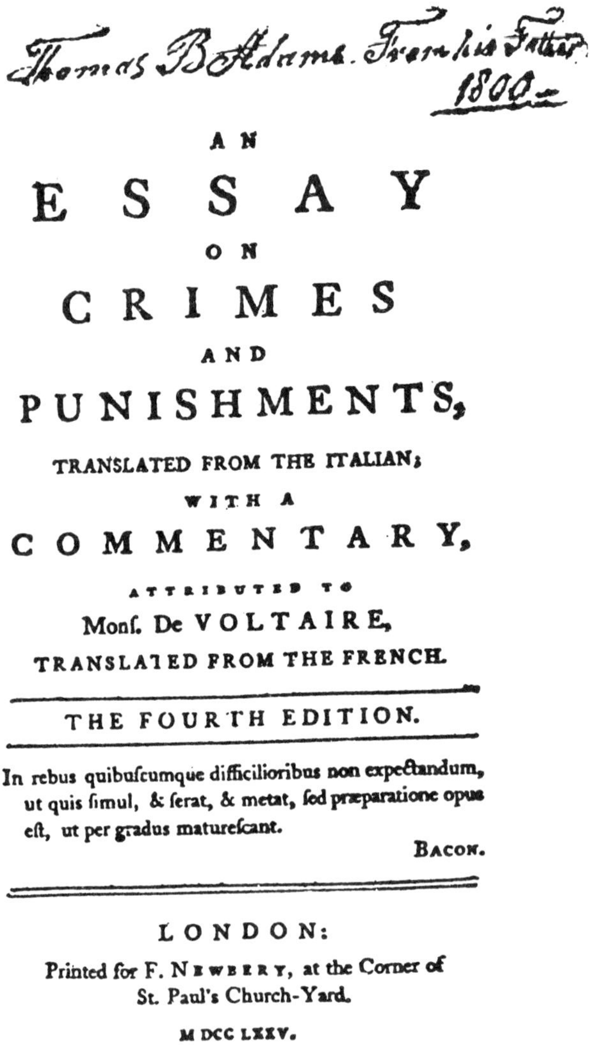

Thomas B Adams. From his Father
1800—

AN

ESSAY

ON

CRIMES

AND

PUNISHMENTS,

TRANSLATED FROM THE ITALIAN;

WITH A

COMMENTARY,

ATTRIBUTED TO

Monſ. De VOLTAIRE,

TRANSLATED FROM THE FRENCH.

THE FOURTH EDITION.

In rebus quibuſcumque difficilioribus non expectandum, ut quis ſimul, & ſerat, & metat, ſed præparatione opus eſt, ut per gradus matureſcant.

BACON.

LONDON:

Printed for F. NEWBERY, at the Corner of St. Paul's Church-Yard.

M DCC LXXV.

Frontespiece of Beccaria's book attributed to Voltaire, given to Thomas B. Adams from his Father John Adams.

ADAMS' COPY OF *On Crimes and Punishments* Comments

One of the earliest translations is the one possessed by John Adams. It was the fourth of its kind, printed in London in 1775 by F. Newbury. In this book, the Coat of Arms of John Adams, stamped on the first page, bears the inscription in Latin: "*Libertatem / Amicitiam / Retinebis / Et Fidem*", which may be translated, "You will retain liberty, friendship, and faith". The name *John Adams*, appears beneath the oval Coat of Arms.

On the title page appears the inscription: "Thomas B. Adams. From his father 1800". This edition, together with an earlier one in Italian, was in the possession of John Adams; and this edition, which he bequeathed to his son Thomas, is in the Rare Book Collection of the Boston Public Library.

It is interesting that in this edition the name of Voltaire appears both on the cover and on the title page of the book. The name of Beccaria, however, appears only in the Preface of the Translator, reprinted from the first edition. The translator, whose name is not known, finds this somewhat peculiar. "With regard to the commentary, attributed to Mons. de Voltaire, my only authority for supposing it his, is the voice of the public, which indeed is the only authority we have for most of his works. Let those who are acquainted with the peculiarity of his manner judge for themselves."

This peculiarity may also explain why the 1777 edition published in Charlestown, South Carolina, has the name of Voltaire and not that of Beccaria, aside from the fact that the American edition of 1777 appears to be a reprint of the London edition. It must also be noted that the same procedure was used for several early Italian editions.

The *Commentary* of Voltaire is divided into twenty three chapters each dealing with a topic treated by Beccaria but expanded by Voltaire, who furnishes examples from situations taking place during that era, and making comparisons on how those situations were dealt with in France, in England, and in Rome during the time of the Empire.

It is difficult to say to what extent the *Commentary* served to promulgate Beccaria's thoughts, as there had already been several editions before Morellet's translation of the Italian into French. The fact that Beccaria's book became widely known under the name of Voltaire is significant at least in the promulgation of those ideas.

Voltaire's *Commentary* is not included in the present edition though it does form the second part of John Adams' copy.

It should further be noted that Adams' copy lacks the chapter, *To the reader*, which took the title of *Preface* in the early Italian editions. Different from Beccaria's final edition is the order of the chapters and heir subdivisions.

AMERICA'S BASIC CHARACTER

Having discovered the route, Christopher Columbus made two continents available first for Europeans and then for the rest of the world. Columbus' character, however, had little if any impact on the character of the Spanish-speaking people of Central and South America; the same can be said for John Cabot--the other Italian--regarding the English-speaking people of North America. The Pilgrims of 1620, on the other hand, gave character and direction to an America yet to be born. Their mark remains indelible to this day.

The manner in which the Pilgrims came (not armed for an invasion), their spirit of independence (daring to govern themselves differently from their people in England), the faith in their religious beliefs (based on a strict moral code), are some of the characteristics that permeate the psyche of the American people. The attribute of fairness, on the other hand, has grown out of the need to co-exist in view of so many immigrants from so many lands and cultures. Except for given individuals who live through cynicism and negativity, and always vociferously active in every society, including that of America, hatred for mankind inexplicably has been and luckily continues to be anathema in the American experience. Respect and benevolence for fellow Americans and a great personal belief in the Creator seem to be reflected in the spirit which has become the conscience of our Founding Fathers. And the documents they created are imbued with the kind of conscience which may best be exemplified in the description that John Adams gives of himself.

In a letter to Thomas Jefferson, Adams makes some interesting observations about the nature of man in general and that of himself in particular:

> Without religion this world would be something not fit to be mentioned in polite company... I believe there is no individual totally depraved. The most abandoned scoundrel that ever existed, never yet wholly extinguished his conscience, and while conscience remains there is some religion...
>
> What shall we think of Virgil and Horace, Sallust Quintillian, Pliny and even Tacitus? and even Cicero, Brutus and Seneca? Pompey I leave out of the question, as a mere politician and soldier. Every one of these great creatures has left indelible marks of conscience and consequently of religion, tho' every one of them has left abundant proofs of profligate violations of their consciences by their little and great passions and paltry interests.
>
> The vast prospect of mankind, which these books have passed in review before me, from the most ancient records, histories, traditions and fables that remain to us, to the present day, has sickened my very soul; and almost reconciled me to Swift's Travels among the Yahoos. Yet, I never can be a misanthrope. **Homo sum**. I must hate myself before I can

> hate my fellow men: and that I cannot and will not do.
>
> No! I will not hate any of them, base, brutal and devilish as some of them have been to me. (From *JOHN ADAMS A Biography in his Own Words* pp. 403-4).

About six months before his death, John Adams contemplated about life: *aut transit, aut finit* (in transition or at an end). Discarding the belief that everything comes to an end--that life is terminal, Adams accepted the belief that it is not terminal--that life is eternal, and that, in his afterlife about to take place, therefore, he would find himself dealing with and under the "administration of [a] Government in the Universe" much as he was under a similar constitutional government he had helped to create during his stay in this world.

BECCARIAN THOUGHTS

- Laws ought to be conventions among men in a state of freedom and have this only end in view: *the greatest happiness of the greatest number.*
- Every act of authority of one man over another, for which there is no absolute necessity, is tyrannical.
- If men are bound to society, society is equally bound to them.
- A sovereign represents society itself and can only make general laws to bind the members of that society.
- Secret accusations make men false and treacherous--whoever suspects another an informer, behold him an enemy.
- Judges have no right to interpret the laws.
- In any government, power is vested in the whole of the people and not in any part of the society.
- The press makes the people, and not few individuals, the guardians and defenders of the laws.
- Every member of society has the right to do anything he or she pleases--provided it is not contrary to the laws--without fearing reprisals of any kind.
- It is an admirable law which ordains that every individual shall be tried by his peers.
- Individuals are innocent until found guilty.
- Judges and/or juries have the responsibility to ascertain, first and foremost, guilt or innocence; if guilty, then the judges and/or juries should take into consideration the extenuating circumstances to decrease or increase the penalties.
- Punishment of a nobleman should not differ from that of the lowest member of society.
- Preservation of life is a natural right; preservation of property is a social right of society.
- Pardons offered to discover associates in crimes have the disadvantages of authorizing treachery.
- A fundamental principle of legislation is the art of conducting men to *maximum* happiness and to *minimum* misery.

BIBLIOGRAPHY

Adams, John. *Diary and Autobiography*. Edited by L. H. Butterfield *et al*. (4 volumes.) Cambridge, MA: Belknap Press, Harvard U. Press, 1961.

_____. *The Earliest Diary of John Adams: June 1753-April 1754, September 1758-January 1759*. Edited by L. H. Butterfield *et al*. Cambridge, MA. Belknap Press, Harvard U. Press, 1966.

_____. *A Biography in His Own Words*. Edited by James Bishop Peabody. New York: Newsweek Book Edition, 1973.

Ambler, Louise Todd. *BENJAMIN FRANKLIN--A Perspective*. Cambridge, MA: Fogg Art Museum, 1975.

AMERICAN ISSUES--The Literary Record. Edited by Willard Thorp. New York: J. B. Lippincott Company, 1941.

Baylin, Bernard. *Ideological Origins of the American Revolution*. Cambridge, MA. Belknap Press, Harvard U. 1967.

Beattie, J. M. *Crime and the Courts in England 1660-1800*. New Jersey: Princeton University Press, 1986.

Beccaria, Cesare. *Opere*. A cura di Sergio Romagnoli. (2 volumes.) Firenze: Sansoni, 1958.

Blackstone, William, Esq. *Commentaries on the Laws of England*. Oxford, 1769.

Caso, Adolph, *TO AMERICA AND AROUND THE WORLD--The Logs of Columbus and of Magellan*. Boston: Branden Publishing Company, 1992.

DOCUMENTS ON FUNDAMENTAL HUMAN RIGHTS. Edited by Zechariah Chafee, Jr. (2 volumes). New York: Atheneum, 1963.

Frutchman, Jack, Jr. *Thomas Paine: Apostle of Free dom*. New York: Four Walls Eight Windows, 1994.

Garrett, Wendel D. *The World of Thomas Jefferson*. New Haven, CT: Barre Publishing Co., 1971.

GREAT ISSUES IN AMERICAN HISTORY: From Settlement to Revolution, 1584--1776. Edited by Clarence L. Ver Streeg and Richard Hofstadter. (2 volumes)--Volume 1 begins with Adam Smith, *Of Colonies* dated 1776, followed by the letter of Columbus to the Queen dated 1694; the first 18 pages of the volume are repeated at the end. New York: Vintage Books, 1969.

ITALIANS AND THE CREATION OF AMERICA, THE. Prepared by Samuel J. Hough. John Carter Brown Library. Providence, RI, 1980.

LETTERS OF DELEGATES TO CONGRESS 1774-1789. Edited by Paul H. Smith. U.S. (3 volumes.) Government Printing Office. Library of Congress, 1976.

Living Documents in American History. Edited by John A. Scott. New York: Washington Square Press, Inc., 1964.

Macy, Jesse. *The English Constitution*. New York: The Macmillan Company, 1898.

Massaro, Dominic R. *Cesare Beccaria--Father of Criminal Justice*. Universitas Internationalis Coluccio Salutati. Cecina, Italy, 1991.

Mayes, Herbert R. *An Editor's Treasury*. (2 volumes.) New York: Atheneum, 1968.

Mazzei, Philip. *MY LIFE & WANDERINGS*. Translated by S. Eugene Scalia, Edited by Margherita Marchione. Morristown, NJ: American Institute of Italian Studies, 1980.

Nordham, George Washington. *George Washington and the Law*. Chicago: Adams Press, 1982.

Padover, Saul K. *The Living U.S. Constitution*. New York: Mentor Books, 1953.

_____. *JEFFERSON*. New York: Harcourt, Brace and Company, 1942.

Plimpton, Ruth Talbot. *MARY DYER--Biography of a Rebel Quaker*. Boston: Branden Publishing Co., 1994.

Powers, Edwin. *CRIME AND PUNISHMENT In Early Massachusetts 1620-1692*. Boston: Beacon Press 1966.

Scull, Florence D. *JOHN DICKINSON SOUNDS THE ALARM*. Philadelphia: Auerbach Publishers, 1972.

THOMAS JEFFERSON--A Biography in His Own Words. The Editors of Newsweek Books. New York: Newsweek, 1974.

UNITED STATES--FORMATION OF THE UNION: DOCUMENTS. Selected, Arranged, and Indexed by Charles C. Transill. U.S. Government Printing Office. Washington, D.C. 1927.

Works of James Wilson, The. Edited by Robert Green McCaskey. Cambridge, MA: The Belknap Press, 1967.

INDEX